I love this book, partly bec[...]
page—my clumsy, halting, [...] walk
with God—but mostly because I recognize the gospel in
almost every page: God's mercy, patience, persistence, and
faithfulness laid out in the most imaginative ways. This
book is a wonderful accomplishment and an excellent read.

FERNANDO ORTEGA, singer-songwriter   *The Rabbit Room*
Story Warren

To read this book is to take a journey. The eyes of your soul
will open widely, and you will blink in wonder at how you
had never seen what you see now. Rebecca Reynolds takes
in hand language, literature, science, philosophy, theology,
and her own life experience to explore those foundational
questions that haunt and confuse us. Enjoy your journey!

SARAH VAN DIEST, author of *God in the Dark: 31 Devotions*
to Let the Light Back In

Wisdom and compassion illuminate every beautiful
sentence of this gospel-infused book. I love that Rebecca
Reynolds chose the title *Courage, Dear Heart*. She's one of
the most courageous people I know, and her heart is one of
the dearest. I hope this is the first of many books from her.

JONATHAN ROGERS, bestselling author

In *Courage, Dear Heart*, Reynolds enters into the depths
of each reader's messy human experience and puts her arm
around them in friendship, offering compassion, wisdom,
and hope. Reynolds speaks to all readers as a close friend,

immersing them in a rich narrative saturated with poetry, literary excerpts, Scripture, and authentic, sometimes painfully honest stories from her life and ministry. *Courage, Dear Heart* is the rare book that not only keeps vigil with readers in the shadows of their struggles but also compassionately walks beside them as they move once again toward the light. I am certain I will return to it many times to experience the grace woven into each paragraph of this wonderful book.

> **JOEL CLARKSON,** author and composer; narrator of The Green Ember audiobook series

Written with imagination and compassion, these letters to a weary world will bring renewed vision and some much-needed courage to their readers.

> **MALCOLM GUITE,** poet and singer-songwriter

Rebecca Reynolds is one of the most perceptive and enjoyable writers I've ever read. In *Courage, Dear Heart,* her exceptional honesty, clarity, and willingness to engage with God in hard things shine through each page. This is not a dry tome. These are word pictures of God and his workings to brighten everyday life.

> **RON BLOCK,** banjoist, guitarist, and vocalist with Alison Krauss & Union Station

Courage, Dear Heart

Courage, Dear Heart

Letters to a weary world

REBECCA K. REYNOLDS

A NavPress resource published in alliance
with Tyndale House Publishers, Inc.

NavPress is the publishing ministry of The Navigators, an international Christian organization and leader in personal spiritual development. NavPress is committed to helping people grow spiritually and enjoy lives of meaning and hope through personal and group resources that are biblically rooted, culturally relevant, and highly practical.

For more information, visit www.NavPress.com.

Courage, Dear Heart: Letters to a Weary World

Copyright © 2018 by Rebecca Reynolds. All rights reserved.

A NavPress resource published in alliance with Tyndale House Publishers, Inc.

NAVPRESS and the NAVPRESS logo are registered trademarks of NavPress, The Navigators, Colorado Springs, CO. *TYNDALE* is a registered trademark of Tyndale House Publishers, Inc. Absence of ® in connection with marks of NavPress or other parties does not indicate an absence of registration of those marks.

The Team:
Don Pape, Publisher
Caitlyn Carlson, Acquisitions Editor
Elizabeth Symm, Copy Editor
Jennifer Phelps, Designer

Published in association with William K. Jensen Literary Agency, 119 Bampton Ct. Eugene, OR 97404

Cover photograph of tape copyright © by cruphoto/Getty Images. All rights reserved.

Cover photograph of brush strokes copyright © by emyerson/Getty Images. All rights reserved.

Author photograph provided by author; used with permission.

Some of the anecdotal illustrations in this book are true to life and are included with the permission of the persons involved. All other illustrations are composites of real situations, and any resemblance to people living or dead is coincidental.

For information about special discounts for bulk purchases, please contact Tyndale House Publishers at csresponse@tyndale.com, or call 1-800-323-9400.

Cataloging-in-Publication Data is Available.

ISBN 978-1-63146-768-4

Printed in the United States of America

24	23	22	21	20	19	18
7	6	5	4	3	2	1

For the Rabbits. All shall be well.

R. K. R.

Contents

Hullo, Out There!: A Note to the Reader

I didn't understand how tired most Christians were until 2007. That year, I was working as a creative coordinator in a church of about two thousand members—a behind-the-scenes dream job for an introvert. At the beginning of every sermon series, the teaching team would talk with me about the main themes they wanted to convey and then invite me to design scripts, props, and visual art for Sunday mornings.

Easter needed to be special, so I talked our pastors into trying something risky. One week before the big service, we passed around baskets full of torn, colored tissue paper and asked our members to write a single word on their chosen piece—a word that captured their biggest sorrow or struggle.

"Keep your word anonymous," I said. "Disguise your handwriting if you don't want anybody to know which one is yours, but be real with whatever you write down. That's important."

My secret plan? To transform these papers into seven eighteen-foot, backlit windows—a massive symbol of God's ability to turn brokenness into beauty. "Trust me," I begged the teaching team. "This is going to be great."

Yet this project that had seemed charmingly simple in my head ended up requiring hours of physical labor. For a week solid I worked, kneeling over huge frames made from wood and vinyl sheeting. Each tiny piece had to be decoupaged so that it fit into a grand design, effort that was close and tedious. On my hands and knees, I read every single paper. *Abused. Cancer. Porn. Shame. Debt. Addict. Loneliness. My sexuality. Obesity. My mom. My son. HIV. Bankruptcy.*

I don't know what Catholic priests feel when they sit listening to parishioners talk through hurt and shame, but I wasn't prepared for the gravity of two thousand confessions. After a decade of ministry, I had expected to read hard words, so I wasn't shocked by the *types* of struggles people admitted. The *volume* of the suffering of the church, though, knocked me flat. I didn't unfold one paper that said *discouraged*— I unfolded two hundred. This single word was written in feminine script, in shaky old handwriting, in masculine block letters, and in teenage bubble letters. All around me, people were carrying terrible burdens. I couldn't keep from crying as I spent those long days alone with the grief of the church, realizing at last that every smiling face I passed in the hallways each week had a story to tell.

The hardest words were written in faint, tiny letters. In these, I saw how difficult it had been to tell the whole truth. Even anonymously, an admission of reality had been terrifying for some. How the Lord must ache as he looks down upon the bare sorrows of his people! With that awareness, the sacrificial system of the Old Testament finally made a little more sense to me. Nothing but fire, smoke, and blood could express the smoldering depths of human pain. The New Testament also rang clearer, since nothing but the infusion of divine life could ever redeem such widespread death. As beautiful as humanity is at times, we are also deeply messed up, too helpless for anything less than the rescue of a God. Never again would I look into a body of Christians with the delusion that most of us were mostly okay.

By Saturday, I had spent close to sixty hours working. My neck was stiff, and every muscle in my body hurt, so when a team of men hung those hulking frames from our sanctuary walls, I could barely lift my chin to see the result. Yet, as they flipped on the backlights, I was floored. It had worked. Two thousand sorrows exploded into bursts of color and light. Cadmium yellow centers, orange and crimson flames, cool recesses of green, pools of blue and violet—could redemption really be so beautiful?

When our worshipers walked into the sanctuary on Easter, they didn't know what we had prepared. But as we lowered the room lights and illuminated the windows, they gasped.

After church was over, they lingered in the sanctuary an hour or more, wandering until they found the tiny words that they had written. Then they looked outward, finding their confession surrounded by the confessions of others and realizing they weren't alone. The whole conversation was entirely anonymous, and yet it felt so intimate.

Friends threw arms around one another and prayed together, whispering. Others stood with their heads bowed. Some knelt. Eventually, the pastors decided to open the church during non-service hours so members could take time to process what we had discovered about ourselves and one another.

In some ways, I was reminded of New Yorkers post 9/11. Do you remember those first desperate hours, how strangers moved toward one another, bleeding and crying, leaning on one another's strength to walk through the rubble? Mass tragedy has a way of exposing our common frailty, and in such intersections of human tenderness and horror, all shields are down. Here we can at last confess, "The world is broken, and I am broken, and my need is dire."

Lonely in a Sea of Faces

When life is going well, most of us keep hacking away at daily life with all our troubles packed deep inside us. Sometimes our stories are too heavy and too complicated to talk about. Maybe we don't think anybody will listen or care, or maybe we've already tried friendships that didn't work. Some of us are working too many hours to even think beyond this week.

So here we are, surrounded by people from early morning till late at night but never really knowing or being known. In fact, Americans are more lonely now than at any point in our national history. According to Janice Shaw Crouse, senior fellow at the Beverly LaHaye Institute, more than one-fourth of Americans claim to "have no one with whom they can talk about their personal troubles or triumphs. If family members are not counted, the number doubles to more than half of Americans who have no one outside their immediate family with whom they can share confidences."[1] Think about that. More than half of us.

This epidemic of loneliness is no respecter of milieu. While we might expect isolation in a big city, even in a tight-knit rural community, it's possible to feel like an outsider. Strong roots grow deep in small groups, but so do scars; if you've ever had to start over at ground zero of a small-town relational breakdown, you know how exhausting that whole process is. You have to get your nerve up to go to the grocery store because there's no telling whom you'll meet in the cereal aisle. Recovering local might make you stronger in the long run, but day in, day out, up-close survival wears you out.

Zooming out a bit more, social media can turn our lives into a lonely flurry of superficial interaction. We post pictures, chat, debate, rant, and empathize. We try to impress. We try to persuade. Yet in the thinness of these constant, disposable connections, the deeper needs of our souls are rarely satisfied. Twenty-four-hour access to dialogue doesn't always equal twenty-four-hour access to true friendship.

One night, I was sitting in my bed, scrolling through social media while my husband sat next to me, reading on his phone. I wish I could tell you that this evening routine is rare for us, but it's not. We both work long hours, and by the end of the day, we're shot. The Internet isn't good for us, but it is easy.

That particular day had been huge in American politics, so hundreds of updates flashed across the screen. In one status, a political figure was honored as a national messiah. In another, he was demonized. In the crossroads of these two opinions, tempers ran high. Here was an earthquake in slow motion; fissures running through friendships, parent-child relationships, and churches. Names were called. Fifth-grade insults were thrown. Accusations were made. Lines were drawn in the sand. Because I love my country dearly, my own heart began to pound, eager to jump in and fight. I wanted to rip every bad argument apart. I wanted to rescue my republic. At the same time, I wanted to run away and hide. Facebook hasn't been the same for me since that election—not since I've learned that it can be a civil war battleground instead of a sidewalk cafe.

It's Complicated

I don't know what's making you weary as you read this book. Some of you are divorced, and some of you secretly wish you were. Some of you hate yourselves because you can't seem to get a grip on food, sex, or your temper. Some of you are recovering from physical or emotional abuse. Maybe you are tired of being single or tired of people classifying you by your relationship status. You could have been asked to leave a job you loved, or maybe you're stuck in a work environment with someone who makes your life miserable. Conflict between friends or family members might have worn you out. You could have an embarrassing disease you are trying to manage. Some of you are choking in financial debt that you are too humiliated to mention. *Abused. Cancer. Porn. Shame. Debt. Addict. Loneliness. My sexuality. Obesity. My mom. My son. HIV. Bankruptcy.* My guess is that some of those words could be your words too.

While shopping at Sam's Club recently, I passed a book written by a badger-grinning televangelist—a man who has made a fortune off promising a healthy, wealthy life to everybody who follows his advice. I needed coffee and was grumpier than normal, so I was punchy. *Stop lying to hurting people so you can sell those stupid books!* I thought.

Bad reaction, I know, but even on caffeinated days, religious teachers like that irk me. Sure, most of us are given some happy seasons of life, but what about the troubles that we would never choose for ourselves? It's easy to praise God some days, but other days, we cry out to him in pain. Doubts about God that we've never wanted to admit may rise to the surface, and we might not feel any sense of direction about what to do next. Some of us will make awful mistakes in this chaos, and the aftermath of our weakness will be troubling and painful. Flashing a big, cheesy smile during such times would actually be more weird than holy, yet so many suffering believers feel pressured to grin and bear it. We don't realize that when the Bible asks us to "rejoice always,"[2] it isn't asking us for an exercise in artificiality.

Even in the midst of writing about peace and joy, Paul wanted to leave this earthly life to go be with Jesus. In fact, he wrote,

> If I go on living in the body, this will mean fruitful labor for me. So what shall I choose? I do not know. I am torn between the two. I desire to depart and be *with Christ*, which is far better indeed.[3]

Paul's use of the words *with Christ* clued me in to something big. His ache was relational, not just geographic. He didn't simply want to get to heaven; he wanted to get further up and further in to community with Jesus. Before catching that, I'd always felt sort of guilty for wanting to escape my earthly life to be closer to the Lord—after all, the Holy Spirit lived inside me. Why couldn't I just be content with what I had already been given? Yet, Paul understood the indwelling of the Holy Spirit better than you or I ever will, and he still longed to experience divine fellowship in a way that was more intimate than anything he could encounter on earth. His story helps me rejoice in all things while admitting the cramp in my side. It gives me permission to live a little homesick.

Paul and I aren't alone in longing for an escape hatch. Do you remember the scene from *The Lion, the Witch and the Wardrobe* in which Aslan asks Lucy and Susan to walk with him before he faces execution? Lewis based this scene on a night when our Lord asked his closest human companions to stay awake with him during an hour of supreme struggle. "My soul is overwhelmed with sorrow to the point of death," said Jesus. "Stay here and keep watch with me."[4] Three times Jesus asked his best human friends to watch with him, and three times those friends let him down. Our Lord wasn't flashing a televangelist's grin during this ordeal; he was alone and grieved to the point of sweating blood. So on those nights when you kneel in the silent dark to pray, wishing for the weight of a friend's arm about your shoulders, you have a Savior who understands what it's like to be without human companionship. Hebrews 4:15 says that "we do not have a high priest who is unable to sympathize with our weaknesses, but one who in every respect has been tempted as we are, yet without sin." So Jesus knows what it means to feel alone. It's shocking that a God would experience this for us; but he loved us enough to take on the troubles of our world.

A couple of months ago, a non-believing friend told me that he loves Greek mythology more than Old Testament stories because Greek gods and goddesses have human personality traits that make them relatable. Zeus is stormy. Hera is manipulative and difficult. Athena plays favorites.

"Holiness is too strange," he said. "I don't understand it. I don't want to be close to a shapeless fire on a mountain."

In this moment, I realized the relational importance of the incarnated Christ because in Jesus, we see a compression of divine emotional complexity. In him, we find a fiery Lord who turns over tables in a temple, a tender Lord who weeps with the weeping, a gentle Lord who welcomes little children, a weary Lord who sleeps, and an introverted Lord who needs time alone.

We also find a Lord who sometimes wants to quit and go home. "Let this cup pass from me,"[5] he prayed—wishing for a way out that would not come. Here, Jesus gives us a beautiful example of authentic prayer—showing us that we don't have to go skipping and grinning into every loss we face. We can cry out. We can weep. We can be honest with the Father about all of our feelings before we come at last to "Not my will, but thine."[6] It's okay for that process to be a monumental battle for us because it was a monumental battle for Jesus. You have a High Priest who is able to empathize. You can talk to him straight.

Words. Presence. Hope.

In this book, I'm going to try to give you three gifts that I have needed during times of weariness. First, I want to offer you clear and strong *words* that describe painful experiences. Why? Because an accurate description of suffering can help us see its boundaries. To feel alone in the pitch dark with a dragon is terrifying—but if we can only light a match, if we can only catch a glimpse of the whole of a threat, we can usually begin to address that monster more strategically.

An accurate description of suffering can also enable us to

find the healing we need. When sorrow knocks us flat, it's hard to find the energy and focus required to unpack our own hearts. But if we can point to someone else's story, this can help us explain our burdens to friends and counselors. Perhaps this is part of the reason God gave us David's psalms: songs modeling honest pain and doubt. Instead of just praising God, David took time to explain his fear and sorrow with utter clarity, allowing readers to say, "Oh! Me too!" David showed us that he understood despair and loss, and this helps us trust him when he went on to claim that God had restored his soul. Without his raw insights on suffering and fear, his joy wouldn't ring as true—the inclusion of both helps us transition from paralysis to praise.

Second, I want to give you the *presence* of a friend who won't freak out about the magnitude of your exhaustion. I sit with you as one who understands weariness on a personal level. If you have failed during seasons of fatigue, know that I have too. During extreme stress, I've made some awful decisions, responding like an animal in pain. A few times, I was even willing to twist my theology to find some sort of relief. I wasn't as strong as I wanted to be, and sometimes those flashbacks of failure still hit me hard. "How could I have been so dense? Why didn't I see that coming? Why didn't I love God more? Why didn't I run away from sin, no matter how much it hurt to run into the dark?"

Yet these same terrible mistakes also showed me the depth of God's love. When he picked me up and carried me in grace, despite the mess I'd made of my faith, he demonstrated a power that is made perfect in human weakness. I'd heard that premise all my life, but I had to see how little strength I had before I could understand how big his love really is. That experience has driven me to reach out to you, hoping and praying that I might be some sort of comfort in the midst of whatever trouble you are experiencing.

Sometimes I make jokes about my best friends being dead writers, but I really do love my favorite authors like family. Until I began writing this book for you, I didn't realize how Lewis, Chesterton, and Tolkien must have prayed for their readers—how they must have sat hunched over unfinished paragraphs, asking the Lord to give them precise words and images that would reach through space and time to fill real human hearts with courage and strength. One of the best parts of writing this book has been understanding how dearly those men must have loved me because now I know how much I've loved you.

So if you feel unseen right now, unwanted, rejected, lost— know that your pain has pulled me through long nights and early mornings of wrestling with these chapters. You are the reason I spent two of the hardest years of my life trying to find honest words for weary people. You are the reason I'm casting a trembling voice out into a critical world. You're worth that risk to me. Even while you've been hurting, I've been praying for you, and I'm praying for you still.

Third, I want to speak *hope* over you. I don't mean that I will give you easy answers, because (despite the movies) God doesn't always zap a long, hard struggle with tactile blessings.

worth that risk

not an expert — speaking from the middle

Yet, the gospel can still refresh our vision in the midst of a difficult journey, filling our lungs with the atmosphere of heaven. It can place a clean, warm cloth on our eyes, fill our bellies with a hearty meal, and invite us to sing old hymns with fellow travelers who remind us why we are doing what we are doing.

These are my three goals for these pages. If you will go with me, I will try to help you look this world in the face, naming it, grieving over it, and finding our Jesus in the midst of it. Because I'm a fellow traveler (not an expert), this book of letters speaks from the middle of discovery, from the middle of a life that still sputters and fumbles. Some days my marriage is messed up. Some days I grieve over parenting mistakes that I would give anything to undo. Some days our finances stress me out. Some days I struggle with unforgiveness, fear, anger, and envy. Some days my theology is wonky. But God is working in my weakness, and he is working in yours. We don't have to be the heroes of our lives. He is.

In C. S. Lewis's *The Voyage of the* Dawn Treader, young Lucy finds herself trapped inside a thick, enchanted darkness in which all nightmares come true. Overwhelmed by fear, she cries out to the great lion: "Aslan, Aslan, if ever you loved us at all, send us help now."[7]

At this moment of desperation, Lucy notices a light. She looks along its beam and sees something inside:

> At first it looked like a cross, then it looked like
> an aeroplane, then it looked like a kite, and at last

with a whirring of wings it was right overhead and was an albatross. It circled three times round the mast and then perched for an instant on the crest of the gilded dragon at the prow. It called out in a strong sweet voice what seemed to be words though no one understood them. After that it spread its wings, rose, and began to fly slowly ahead, bearing a little to starboard. . . . No one except Lucy knew that as it circled the mast it had whispered to her, "Courage, dear heart," and the voice, she felt sure, was Aslan's, and with the voice a delicious smell breathed in her face.[8]

So courage, dear heart. I know you are tired. I know the darkness is thick and the way is longer and harder than you ever expected it to be. But God sees you, he hurts with you, and he welcomes your honesty. Even to the ends of the earth, he will lead you on.

I Know a Stranger: A Letter to the Rejected

Leah's never been beautiful like her baby sister.[1] If those two girls had been born boys, the difference wouldn't have mattered so much, but even before they were four and seven, they were divided into the two categories all women learn— the Pretty One and the Ugly One.

Leah survived the comparison as best as she could. She spent her twelfth and thirteenth summers sitting on metal bleachers, reading Asimov, waiting for Rachel to finish Little Miss Paddan-aram competitions. On the night Rachel was crowned homecoming queen, Leah stood on the sidelines and clapped. "Congrats to your sister," a couple of football players said. People always talked to Rachel through her.

After twenty-two years of this, Leah should have known

better than to take a second look when a handsome new guy showed up in town. Still, before she could stop it, a flutter of *maybe-he's-different?* rose up in her chest. Hope hit before she could throw up her defenses, before she remembered why he would never even see her. Men don't look for the moon while the sun is blazing.

Of course, Jacob decides to hang around for a while after he gets an eyeful of Rachel, and the whole time he is goofy, tripping over himself in love.

"Tell her I'm crazy about her," he says to Leah.

"Yeah, yeah. Whatever."

"Tell her!" he begs.

"Crazy about her?" she mumbles. Leah knows crazy. She's the crazy *Star Trek* fan, the crazy book nerd, the crazy stand-up comic who knows how to deflect pain with a laugh. Lately, she's becoming the crazy cat lady and the crazy, single twentysomething who shows up at other people's baby showers and other people's weddings.

But then, no. Suddenly, she's not the spectator.

She wakes up one morning and finds out that her dad has arranged the rest of her life for her. Leah tells him she won't do it—that she's not okay with being treated like this—but her father threatens her within an inch of her life. Leah doesn't have anywhere to go. She doesn't have anywhere to turn.

Rachel gets wind of the plan and comes unglued. "He's *mine, you ugly thing*! He'll *never* love you!" she screams, and the servants drag her kicking and yelling to wait in the desert until the wedding is final. Leah finds a bottle of wine and drinks too much, hoping to numb her dignity.

After the ceremony, Leah is taken to Jacob's pitch-black tent, where, for one night, she finds out what it is like to be wanted. In the dark, she could be anybody, and she hears praises roll off her husband's tongue—"You are so beautiful. So perfect." As he whispers over her, he tells her that he would have worked twice as long for this, and then he sleeps with his hand on the bare turn of her hip.

Dawn breaks with a shout.

"The ugly one! You gave me the ugly one! Where is my real wife? Where is the woman I wanted?"

He rages while Leah is still sore, still shy, still naked from the only night she would ever be more than an obligation to him. She pulls the sheet over her shoulder and turns away, numb.

Jacob protests until he gets Rachel, too, and from the day her sister walks in the door, Leah could have walked in front of the television naked and her husband wouldn't have seen her. No, Leah is the utilitarian wife, the one who runs to the CVS at 11:30 p.m. to pick up a gallon of milk.

"Can you get that, Leah?" Rachel whines, commanding as much as asking when the phone rings, and Leah dries her hands on the dish towel. Jacob is sitting on the sofa, flipping channels on the remote; Rachel's head is on a pillow in his lap. He's playing with a curl of her pretty hair.

When Jacob comes to Leah, the work of sex isn't gently done. Here is a farmer who breeds sheep strategically, who sows crops on rotation. He impregnates his first wife mechanically, checking the moon and planting his seed like a man driving a tractor. Still, Leah's first boy is born with his father's hands and chin, and when she notices this, she thinks her heart will explode. Labor was rough, and her doctor says she isn't supposed to walk yet, but Leah folds cloths together to staunch the blood and finds her feet. She carries her boy to his papa to claim the bond that binds them.

"Behold, a son! He is Reuben," she says as she hands him over, thinking, *Surely Jacob will love me now.* He pulls the swaddling back, checks the boy over, and is glad to see that the umbilical cord is cut clean.

Six months later, it's time to grow the farm again. Cracking his back, Jacob sits on Leah's bed to kick off his work boots. The last deed of the day is quickly done, then he walks out of the room, saying, "Clean out the van tomorrow, Leah. I need to take it to the shop."

But Leah can't sleep, so she doesn't wait until morning. She pulls on sweat pants and her NASA hoodie, and she walks into the cool night air, where she cries her eyes out, stuffing empty water bottles and plastic wrappers into an old grocery bag. Then she sits in the driver's seat and weeps, beating her fists against the steering wheel while *the God who hears* stirs a second son to life inside her.

Simeon is born with his father's feet and his mother's ears, but Leah takes it easy after labor this time, tracing the lines of his little face while he sucks at her breast. Jacob will see him when he sees him. No need to rush.

A third harvest, then Levi. *Three sons are lucky,* Leah thinks. *One of these days, he's going to see how I do him good; he's going to see how I'm his good-luck charm; he's going to want me close. He is a farmer, and I am a producer; I cannot be dismissed.*

But Rachel hears the new baby's cry, and she sulks and weeps until Jacob takes her off to a pretty hotel in the mountains and buys her a monogrammed bathrobe and roses to carry home in a blue glass vase. She refuses to speak to Leah for three months.

Two more years pass. Leah's body is ruined. She has stretch marks and a belly paunch, varicose veins, fat on her hips, fat on her legs. It doesn't matter. Fat or thin, worn or new, it is all the same to Jacob. He never looks. Never feels. So when Judah is born, Leah throws all four boys in the van and drives to the beach solo. She wears a Land's End swim dress and a floppy-brimmed hat, slathers on SPF 50, and doesn't care who sees her. Then she stands in the tide up to her knees, watching the waves shake the fat on her thighs, and says, "This time I will praise the Lord."

Leah has good boys who love their mother, especially Reuben, who probably carries too much. He has watched his mom's cheeks turn pink when the pregnancy test comes back positive, watched her sing while doing the housework, watched her fly, and then watched her crash. He knows the mandrake is supposed to bring more sons, and he knows how his mother carries children inside her like music she is writing, so he pulls the plant out by its roots and runs to her, saying, "Mama, Mama, it will all work out somehow." Leah holds his head to her belly and bends over to kiss him.

Rachel sees it all. Desperate for a child of her own, she wants that mandrake. She holds her pretty hand out and demands it.

"You want my mandrake?" Leah says slowly. Then, without deciding to do it, she lets fly everything she has always wanted to say to her sister: "You're such a spoiled brat— a beautiful little spoiled brat. You expect everybody to coddle and serve you, don't you? You took my husband, and now you want to take the gift my own son brings me?"

Shock on Rachel's face. The beginning of the rosebud pout she wielded as a baby. But Leah shows her no softness this time.

"Please, Leah. Just give it to me," Rachel begs, threatening to rage.

Leah stays calm. "You want this? A trade then. One night. One night with Jacob." A deal among sisters, among wives— a financial transaction.

Leah doesn't bother to fix her hair or put on makeup when she walks out to the garage to tell him. Jacob's slid himself under a car, changing the oil. "You will sleep with me tonight," she tells him, as businesslike as he has ever been with her. This time Leah is in control. This time she calls the shots. "I have paid for your services. Your stud fee." And then, because there is nothing more to discuss, she turns and walks back inside. That night she undresses like a woman in an OB-GYN exam room. It will be over soon enough.

Leah names this boy Issachar so that every time her husband speaks the boy's name, he will be confessing that God evens the score.

A new son. Zebulun, the gift of God. With this boy, Leah cries out in honest pain, "I have given him all these sons. What has been my crime? Did I decide to be born ugly? Wouldn't I have chosen anything other than being trapped inside a body like this?"

I want Leah's story to get easier, but it doesn't—at least not in the way I expect. Rachel dies in childbirth, leaving Jacob devastated. What is Leah supposed to do with this? Does she rush to comfort him? Would he even want her around? As Leah listens to her husband mourn, she has to know that he would rather have lost her instead. Besides this, suddenly her two nephews don't have a mom. One of them is a squawling newborn. She'll have to help take care of those boys while watching her husband coddle them, talking constantly about the beauty of their mother.

As the kids get older, the internal pressure grows. Leah's first son, Reuben, makes the stupid mistake of sleeping with his father's girlfriend—not good for family relations. Her grandchildren goof things up too, and Leah grieves as she watches tension build between her sons and the sons of Rachel. Everything is awkward. Everything is uncomfortable. Nothing is as it should be, and she can't ever seem to get away from it all.

Like a kite caught in rough winds, Leah twists and turns on the strings that bind her. Every time she gets the courage to move toward her husband, she ends up shrinking away from him. Then, when she finally says, "Forget Jacob; I'm going to praise God," she stumbles in her faith. (Don't we all?) She grieves. She maneuvers. She lashes out. She takes a few more steps; it's all so messy. Only in burial is she united with the husband who has never wanted her, and I can't tell if the Bible is hinting at resolution by including this detail or if it's showing us the irony of the situation.

It hurts to read Leah's story, but that's part of the reason I love it. The Bible tells the truth unflinchingly—nothing has been cleaned up; nothing has been patched over. Leah's story is brutal because rejection is brutal. If you've lived through it, you know that already.

A Hundred Shades of Rejection

No matter how rejection hits, realizing that you are unwanted is awful. I don't know what happened to you. Maybe an aging parent openly rejected you. Maybe your spouse of twenty-five years left you for someone younger. Maybe your best friend walked away. Maybe a church disaster left you alone in the spiritual wilderness. Any *one* of these experiences can knock you to your knees, but when rejection hits over and over again from different angles—as it has for some of you—it can become hard to believe that anybody could ever love you again.

I'm almost embarrassed to tell you how I thought Christian relationships worked when I was in my twenties.

During these years, I was reading stacks of complex theology books, gaining my first *intellectual* grasp on the mechanics of the gospel. I was elated to realize that we truly were "saved by grace, not by works,"[2] and I assumed that every person working for a reputable ministry would operate according to this principle.

Giddy at the thought of an expansive grace, I confessed my mistakes quickly (even my ugliest and stupidest mistakes) and waited for my leaders to pull me back to the truth of Christ's power over my sin. Like a freckled kid who belly flops off the high dive, I fell eagerly, giving my trust to pastors, to small-group leaders, and to members of my cell groups. Because I was expecting gospel community to catch me, I was shocked when it did not. My leaders needed the same grace I did, but I was a young Christian who didn't realize how dependent we all remain on the constant resources of Jesus.

One day, I accidentally overheard some of my ministry leaders talking about new staff recruits (of which I was one). Apparently, all the newbies had been ranked by number, most to least valuable. I still don't know if I understood that flash of dialogue correctly, but in those few seconds, I got the impression that I was at the bottom of their list—the least likely staff member to make an impact for the gospel on campus. That shard of identity wouldn't leave me alone. I thought about it a hundred times and eventually decided that such an assessment of my ability made sense. I didn't have the network of a sorority. I wasn't blonde. I wasn't cute. I was just an average plebe, a little artsy, a lot nerdy. I wore sweatshirts instead of oxfords. I needed to lose fifteen pounds. I didn't have the social poise to waltz into a dorm full of lost girls and rustle up a trail of giddy new disciples. Yeah. They were right about me. I couldn't do much for the Kingdom. I was on the B-team.

This single overheard (and possibly misheard) comment made a huge impact on my heart. Every time I failed, I thought about it. Every time I sat in a staff meeting, I felt tolerated instead of needed. Knowing that God's people had a ranking system made me wonder if Jesus saw things this way. Maybe this ministry had put me on the bottom rung because God had too.

The Greatest Lie

I knew better than to believe this. On paper, I could prove that God loved me and that he wasn't limited by any of my weaknesses. In fact, during one of my theology courses, a prof had used a simple train diagram to show us how to manage our insecurity. This diagram showed an engine labeled "facts," a car labeled "faith," and a caboose labeled "feelings," and I was told that if I would just place my "faith in the facts, the feelings would follow." I tried so hard to make this work for me, but when it took months or years for the "right" feelings to kick in, I began to grow ashamed. This formula looked so easy on paper—if it wasn't working, I must be at fault somehow.

Now that I'm older, however, I know how long it can take for human emotions to align with truth. *Feeling* is a complicated process rooted in the slow time of relationship, and repairing emotions is not usually a quick fix. *Intellectual knowledge* of good theology isn't a magic wand, and repairing a sense of rejection can be particularly hard. When we harbor the insidious belief that we don't please the God who has promised to love us, when we don't *feel* as if God wants us, regardless of any truths we have memorized, everything trembles.

About eighteen years ago, an acquaintance of mine was telling me about her morning quiet time. In a reverent whisper, she said, "Don't you just love how *he* shows up when we take time to meet with him?" She described a glimmer of sunlight on the rim of her teacup, and I felt my face flush. No, my quiet times didn't feel like what she was describing. Once I drank a Surge cola before a Bible study at 8:30 a.m., and for a few seconds, I thought I might be having some sort of transcendental experience. But those goose bumps were high-octane caffeine. That's it. No more.

By telling you that, I don't mean to make light of legitimate interactions with the Lord. I have experienced moments of true, felt intimacy with God—flashes of eternal warmth and wild longing—awe over his holiness—intermittent surges of feeling at once at home and homesick. But these glimpses of God's presence can feel devastatingly few and far between when you are waiting for another one to hit. Though focused time in Bible study and prayer generally lead to a sense of greater spiritual intimacy, God isn't a vending machine. During a few strange years (which I still struggle to understand), reading the Bible became dry and difficult for me; every study session seemed to turn up another paradox or snag. As a result, I began to dread opening the text. I didn't feel as if I could admit this to a church that immediately affiliated spiritual drought with sin or unbelief. Not until reading chapter 8 of C. S. Lewis's *Screwtape Letters* did I see that God could be intentional about the silent, "trough seasons" of our faith, a concept that helped me relax again in the mercy of God. Now I believe that tactile evidence of God's presence can depend more on what the Far Country wants to show me than on what I want to see for myself. But during those years when I was digging hungrily around in commentaries, insecure about God's love for me, wanting to feel close every minute of every day, I could not understand why he didn't rush in large and loud to save the day.

So hearing that the Lord made regular appearances with a woman so poised, so thin, so perfect—someone who always knew which clothes to buy and how to decorate her house— that hurt. I felt as if I were stumbling into the rank system all over again. The world had already shown me a thousand ways I wasn't good enough, and now I had to admit that the God I claimed to love hadn't doted on me as he seemed to be doting on others. As I listened to this woman revel in her spiritual delights, all my fears calcified. Why would God want a bumbling dork like me when he could hang out with her?

I didn't talk about that to anybody. I felt too ashamed, too afraid of the reality it suggested. The enemy of my soul wanted me to keep my sense of rejection in the same place he corrals all human fears—trapped in that vague, damning silence he uses to breed maximum harm. So as best as I could, I kept working for the Kingdom, hoping that if I gave up enough for Jesus, jumping through enough hoops, I would eventually matter to him too.

In Sunday school classes, we teach our kids to sing "Jesus loves me!" but as we grow up and engage with a broken church, that simple promise can become incredibly hard to believe. God's love is packed into doctrinal statements and sermons, but does it saturate the practical machinery of the body? We hear Christian songwriters on the radio singing love songs for the plain-faced. We follow bloggers who travel to the depths of the third world (or the inner city) to take selfies with the deformed and the desperate. But offstage, some people are special and some are not. Even if no one says it out loud, in subtle ways the church implies, "You must be a gifted speaker, a lovely singer, a physically beautiful person, or a charismatic leader to matter."

Where does this problem begin? I'm not sure. Maybe it begins with church consultants who divide Christian leadership roles into alpha and beta qualities. Promoting CEO traits over the teacher/shepherd qualities (the latter of which the Bible clearly calls us to follow) can cause church dialogue to shift away from a gospel core to trust in persona, labels, statistics, annual plans, and ten-year goals.

Strategic planning isn't inherently wrong, of course, but good things do have a way of taking over the best things, and secular priorities in leadership will trickle down into the values of the body as a whole, creating a church culture that rings of TED Talks and John Maxwell more than the Good News of Jesus. The influential and the lovely gain visibility, leadership, and people to marry while Average Joe and Average Jill pass in and out of church doors without anything too brilliant to say, and without a wound exotic enough for anyone to notice. In a dynamic like this, how are the Leahs of our world supposed to develop a radical vision of God's love for them?

The Audacity of a Second-Class Hope

In Song of Solomon chapters 1 and 2, we find a second Leah figure who brings the first Leah's story full circle. In one of the sweetest, most moving parallels of the Bible, we learn that one of Leah's great-great-great (etcetera) grandsons has fallen in love with a woman who is very much like her.

This woman is a Shulamite, someone who doesn't match up to the beauty standards of her time. She's also insecure because her own family has rejected her. Her brothers have turned her into a slave, making her work in the fields until abuse and physical labor have taken a toll on her face and figure.

"Do not gaze at me because I am dark,"[3] she appeals to the king. Her skin is rough and worn out. Her nails are torn. Her hair is dry, frayed by the hard sun. Her own family has driven her so hard, she hasn't been able to take care of her own body.

Imagine how intimidating this situation would be. A *king* is pursuing her, the sort of man other women want. His hallways are full of celebrities—tall, lithe beauties with money, leisure, clothes, and cosmetics. They know what to say. They know what to wear. They know when to laugh. The Shulamite doesn't even want to lift her head in such an elegant place. Surely, it would be impossible for a king to love an overworked, rugged farm girl.

I don't know how the Shulamite resists running away from him; but in fact, she does the opposite. Smack in the middle of her deepest inadequacy, she confesses something so delicate, it makes me nervous to read. Though she feels worn out, unlovable, ugly, the Shulamite admits that she wants to be pursued—not just by any man, but by royalty.

Her dream is the desire of every rejected soul, though few of us have the courage to admit it after years of disappointment. It's so much easier to become cynical. Still, the Shulamite knows her own heart well enough to know exactly what she wishes her lover would say: "Arise, my love, my beautiful one, and come away. O my dove, in the clefts of the rock, in the crannies of the cliff, let me see your face, let me hear your voice, for your voice is sweet, and your face is lovely."[4]

Of all things, she wants him to think that she is beautiful. This confession is so audacious, so tender, so dangerous, my heart races at every word. I feel protective. I want to shield the Shulamite from her own vulnerability. "Honey, be careful," I find myself whispering. "What if he doesn't want you?" Yet she doesn't cower. She gets brave, and she gets honest, and she disrobes the truth of her heart in the broad daylight.

In the end, she finds out that the rejection of others hasn't prevented the king from loving her. In fact, he is so crazy about the Shulamite, he writes one of the most beautiful poems in all of Scripture to celebrate her beauty. Does this story give us a hint about how the rejected souls of earth are received by their heavenly Bridegroom? Is it a coincidence that the DNA of Leah ran through the veins of a king who adored a rejected Shulamite? And is it a coincidence that the DNA of Leah runs through the veins of the King of kings who adores you and me? It's a little bit scary to hope like this, isn't it? It feels like too much to wish for.

If you have read the Narnia books, you might remember the chapter in which Lucy and Susan are finally allowed to embrace Aslan. It would be frightening to touch a lion— even a good one. (Maybe especially a good one.) Yet in all of his glory and power, Aslan does not reject the girls. Though he is more beautiful than they are, he doesn't shun their ache to love and be loved by him. He lets the girls be close. Then, after Aslan's death and resurrection, their union grows even sweeter. He is not just approachable; he is playful:

"Oh, children, catch me if you can!" He stood for a second, his eyes very bright, his limbs quivering, lashing himself with his tail. Then he made a leap

Chesterton quote

high over their heads and landed on the other side of the Table. Laughing, though she didn't know why, Lucy scrambled over it to reach him. Aslan leaped again. A mad chase began. Round and round the hill-top he led them, now hopelessly out of their reach, now letting them almost catch his tail, now diving between them, now tossing them into the air with his huge and beautifully velveted paws and catching them again, and now stopping unexpectedly so that all three of them rolled over together in a happy laughing heap of fur and arms and legs. It was such a romp as no one has ever had except in Narnia; and whether it was more like playing with a thunderstorm or playing with a kitten Lucy could never make up her mind. And the funny thing was that when all three finally lay together panting in the sun, the girls no longer felt in the least tired or hungry or thirsty.[5]

As long as I have ever wanted anything, I have wanted this closeness—but while that story makes my heart pound, it also makes me realize how much I fear rejection. I want to rush to embrace my King, and yet, I hesitate.

The Wanted Ones

"A thing must be loved *before* it is loveable," Chesterton wrote.[6] He said this was the great theme of *Beauty and the Beast*—a story that is magical not because a beautiful princess

31

gets kissed (after all, beautiful women are kissed every day) but because a hideous monster is embraced while he is still a hideous monster.

By the time Belle shows up at the Beast's castle, he can't hope to be wanted by anybody. He's too wretched. Too damaged. Each time the Beast begins to approach vulnerability, he shrinks back with the lonely despair of a human who believes that he could never be loved. Yet the Christ figure of the story, Belle, is determined to cross that gulf. Her grace displays a magic greater than any fairy godmother's bibbidi-bobbidi-boo because she is showing us a metaphor for the gospel: "God shows his love for us in that while we were still sinners, Christ died for us."[7] He pursued us while we were still ugly Leah, still worn-out Shulamite, still Average Jill.

God brought me face-to-face with his preemptive love during the early days of our adoption. In that first stage of the process, we had no name, no photograph, no idea which child would be ours, and I was scared. The stakes were high, after all. We were committing the rest of our lives, the whole of our family, to a kid we didn't know.

Still, the feeling that someone was out there waiting for us persisted. Eventually, I started having a recurring dream in which I was standing behind a barrier of yellow, sound-proof glass, watching fifteen or twenty babies crawling on the floor in an industrial-looking room. Furnishings were sparse—a bare table, a steel chair, a light bulb hanging by a wire. I could see the kids, but I couldn't hear them, and that silence was awful.

A dark-eyed child with close-cut hair sat still and stared up at me. He scooted my direction and lifted his arms as if he wanted me to hold him, so I walked the length of the wall, trying to find the edge. Yet the further I walked, the thicker the glass grew. Desperate to reach him, I finally reared back and threw my shoulder against the wall, trying to break it, and that's when the dream would end. I would lurch upright in bed, covered in sweat, then stumble to my laptop in the dark to search adoption agency websites.

In those early hours, I would scroll through profiles of waiting children, reading cases listed by snapshots. Some kids were natural charmers with big smiles and mischief in their eyes. Others looked vacant, wounded, or defiant. What are you supposed to do with that difference as an adoptive parent? Every kid takes a weird picture now and then—once my oldest son decided to scowl through an entire family wedding. If another mom saw only one image from that event, what would she think of my son? Would she assume that he had anger issues? Would she write him off as a tough case? How was a waiting child supposed to understand that his or her entire future might hinge on a two-second snapshot?

One of the boys stared wide-eyed into the camera, looking dazed. I wondered if he ever laughed—or if he didn't, what it would take to help him learn how. A pretty little girl with fat, red cheeks had an easy, open grin that promised she would melt seamlessly into any family. Her foster parents must have adored her because she was dressed like a princess. Three gangly tweens made peace signs with their fingers, but hunched shoulders betrayed their insecurity. A child with a burned face wouldn't lift his chin.

On one website, children were labeled by an American nickname plus a medical condition. Lucy—Spina bifida. Charlie—Hepatitis. Margaret—Clubfoot. A label like that would open or close doors because certain adoptive families waited years for the youngest possible baby with no medical problems. One of my biological kids was born with a heart defect, and my husband was born with a clubfoot, so it offended me to see people *like us* described as specimens. And yet, did we have the resources to care for every child I wanted to bring home? No. Parents pursuing special-needs adoptions will often tell you that the hardest part of the whole process is sitting at your kitchen table, filling out the checklist that separates the medical conditions you can provide for from those you can't. Every box you don't check feels like a son or daughter lost.

I was overwhelmed and scared in so many ways during those months—scared of being too reckless and scared of being too careful. But in that emotional tug-of-war, our calling was eventually solidified. Longing to be with our son began to outweigh my fears of making a mistake. As the thought of our boy became real, I prayed for every finger, every toe, every bone, every memory. Appeals to the Father rose from me like contractions.

It's crazy looking back on all that now. Seven years have passed, and today is a lazy Saturday morning at our house. Our youngest son is playing in the next room over. He's singing a made-up tune with made-up words, and he is so chilled out and peaceful, the sound of his voice makes me a little sleepy. How did we ever live without him? Why was I ever so afraid?

Before we brought M home, I heard other families joke about forgetting that their kids had been adopted, but that seemed impossible. How could you forget something like that? Now that I've been through it, though, I get what those parents meant. Regular life kicks in, and you spend hundreds of days doing what families do. You read stories; you pack lunches. You go to ball games and swimming lessons. "That kid" becomes "your kid," so that when you see little brown legs running across the lawn, they feel familiar and right— even if your own legs are pink. Of course, I never forget all the paperwork and travel required to adopt M, but a parallel emotional reality runs alongside those memories—a reality in which we seem to have always been together.

On the hot summer day when we finally met our son, I buried my nose in his sweaty black hair, breathed him in, and was shocked to realize that he smelled like one of my own. Even his weight was familiar. I hadn't expected that. I had been told that our transition would take months of getting used to one another, that he would feel foreign and different—but from first contact, this was already my boy.

He was barely three years old that day, and for about a minute, he screamed at the newness of being handed to a strange family. But when he saw that we had Teddy Grahams and Play-Doh, he was ready to have some fun. The big kids sat down to play with him, and those three were soon a big mess of giggles. Our oldest son taught M that his big sister's name was "Grandma." When his sister protested in shock, M got the joke and pushed it: "Grandma! Grandma! Grandma!" Two brothers ganging up on the sister. Weird sense of humor. Yeah, this was going to be a perfect fit. The first day of an adoption isn't always like this, and stories of tenacious love are beautiful in a different way. But for whatever reason, our bond was cake.

Experts had told us not to give our son rich foods after bland orphanage fare, but when we stepped off the bus near our hotel, we saw a McDonald's, and I caved instantly. "Diarrhea, schmiarrhea," I said. "Let's get ice cream." He dipped his fries in his cone, humming with delight, and I thought I was going to explode from happiness watching him. Finally, he was close. Finally, I could relax. Here was the child of our long labor—the son that the Lord had buried deep in my heart was now at my side.

But as beautiful as those early days were, we also began to notice an odd pattern. M rarely cried when he was hurt or sad. When he felt upset, he would either hide behind a chair until he collected himself or put on a goofy performance to make everyone (including himself) laugh. Sure, this was cute, but something about it didn't feel right.

I started working through a list of bonding exercises, just to see if they would help M relax more completely. A social worker had told me to gently wrap M in soft blankets, giving him a sippy cup while rocking him like a baby. (Apparently, muscles used in swaddled sucking grow connections in the brain.) I wore a tank top and held his skin against my arms and neck for long stretches. I counted his toes over and over, playing the piggy game. We crawled on our knees like babies, and I massaged his legs and arms with lotion after a bath. We played in water, dug our arms down deep in rice, and smeared around finger paints. With slow intentionality, we walked back through all the stages of infancy, one day pretending that M was a month old, then two months old, then six. We asked God to help us heal what had been lost.

In certain overseas orphanages, caregivers aren't allowed to snuggle with infants. The no-contact rule is enforced because held babies cry to be held more, and crying babies make more work for facility workers. The world's worst orphanages have rooms with beds full of silent infants because those children have learned that no comfort will come to them when they wail. Of course, such isolation is damaging. God made the needs of babies and the instincts of mothers to work in harmony. When a mother plays with her baby's pretty feet or smooths his soft hair, she is helping his brain understand its relationship to his body. A child who doesn't have this sort of contact cannot develop that understanding properly. This is why children who aren't held in the beginning of life sometimes wiggle constantly, banging into the world around them. They are looking for the edges of themselves.

Our son spent his first year of life in a facility that forbade snuggling, so we found an occupational therapist who taught us joint compressions and impact-oriented exercise.

She encouraged us to spend afternoons jumping off walls, tumbling, wrestling, and working M's bones. In the evenings, we would sit close together reading books. Through all of this, the soul that had been locked inside our son began to break free.

One afternoon, M was climbing into bed when he fell off the mattress onto the floor. Falling is normal for a three-year-old, but what came out of M that day wasn't normal. He let out the halted wail of a newborn. I ran to him, and he looked at me as if he wasn't sure what was happening. When I scooped him up and held him in my arms, he buried his face in my shoulder and wept. My husband heard the commotion and found us.

"What happened?" he mouthed.

"I think this is a good thing," I whispered back.

Almost immediately, I felt my son's shame rise, and he began fighting his tears. His whole body started to stiffen, so I held him closer and told him, "I love you. You are such a good boy. This is a good cry. You are doing a good job crying! Cry more."

One of the best compliments of my life was his decision to take me up on that offer. M relaxed and wept what felt like three years' worth of tears. "I am so proud of you," I said, rocking him and whispering praise and love over him until he was finished.

When all the tears were gone, the look in his eyes told me that he wasn't sure what had just transpired. So I got out my laptop and searched for videos of newborns crying while their mothers comforted them. M was enchanted. As those tiny babies whimpered and wailed, I stroked the screen and said, "Good baby. Good cry." With a little fat finger, my son also began to stroke the faces on the screen. He leaned over to kiss those babies, saying, "Good baby, good cry." Every time a video ended, he asked to watch it again. From that day on, M cried when he needed to cry. He stepped bravely out of the rejection of his past, trusting his family with the reality of his pain.

Before M, I didn't understand what fierce love God holds for those he has adopted into his family. I didn't realize that when he pursues us, he knows all our damage and our defects—and he knows exactly where we rank on every system humans use to determine our value. He stares straight into all of the world's opinions of us and yet proclaims that we are the *wanted ones*. No matter how anybody has let us down, hurt us, forgotten us, we are still longed for and beloved children.

Some of you will find this hard to believe because you have been labeled by your wounds and rejected. You have been judged by snapshots taken on your worst days and left alone to survive. For years, you've sat in the cinders, weeping, and no handsome prince has ever popped in to propose to you. On long, cold nights, you have fallen asleep in the ashes while trying to stay warm, and in the mornings, you have awakened filthy. By day, you have busted your bones working, only to get the tar beaten out of you. You've worn yourselves down. You've worn yourselves ugly.

You've learned to hide behind a chair, or find some way to make people laugh, or pretend to need nothing at all. After surviving so much for so long, how can you hope for anything else?

If that's the case, maybe reaching for the full promise of the gospel is too much too soon. Maybe for now, you can just let the bonds of trust begin to grow between you and your Jesus. If you are wary of giving your whole heart away to him, dig around in his story, and get to know this person who lived as a broken man among broken men. Read about the night he stood alone in the dark after all his friends ran away, and read about the day he stood in front of a hateful crowd that shouted, "Give us Barabbas."[8] See how he grieved, and was lonely, and got tired sometimes.

Seven hundred years before Jesus' birth, the prophet Isaiah described the earthly life of the Messiah this way:

He had no form or majesty that we should
        look at him,
    and no beauty that we should desire him.
He was despised and rejected by men,
    a man of sorrows and acquainted with grief;
and as one from whom men hide their faces
    he was despised, and we esteemed him not.
Surely he has borne our griefs
    and carried our sorrows;
yet we esteemed him stricken,
    smitten by God, and afflicted.[9]

So when you pray, you pray to someone who knows how it feels to be unattractive and abandoned. You pray to someone whose life was so full of hurt that he was called a "man of sorrows." He was hated so much, people hid their faces from him. He was so disgraced, the public thought he was smitten by the hand of God.

When the world tells you that you don't deserve love, know that this accusation landed inside Jesus. When it tells you that you are too plain, too fat, too addicted, too old, too slow, too damaged—believe that he knows the blunt force of every word. And unlike all the humans you've known, he isn't the least bit discouraged by your homeliness. He knows that "a thing must be loved before it is loveable," and he knows that loving you into beauty is *his* business. In fact, he loved you long before your first rejection.[10] Even before the creation of the world, he had a vision of the glorious being he would make of you—someone who is "holy and blameless in his sight."[11] When he looks at you, he sees what you will become, not just what you have been.

In other words, the fairy tales are true—you don't have to be pretty, you don't have to be smart, you don't have to be important—you can come as a child of the cinders, only courageous enough to admit that you are tired of rejection and that you desperately need an affection that the world has never quite been able to give you.

Just as it was difficult for my son to learn to trust his mother, it's going to be difficult for you to learn to trust the God who loves you. It's okay if you have to go slowly and test to see who he really is before you leap. But at the end of this journey, I can tell you what awaits by telling you how my heart sang when my son finally found the courage to bury his sorrows in his mother's love. In that moment, I could feel the love of his God coursing through me toward him—a Father who wants every orphaned soul to collapse in hope on his shoulder. This is the God who loves you. This is the God who chases you. And when you are ready to trust him, he will hold you close and whisper that you are home at last.

Bird with a Broken Wing: A Letter to the Long-Suffering

She told me about a line of locust trees that stood outside her bedroom. On the first day that he hurt her, she said, her mind left her body to climb those branches so she could hide far off the earth—so far that she wouldn't feel anything at all. When her father hit her mother in the kitchen, she hid behind the living-room couch and traced the upholstery pattern with her finger. It was one of those old-school, bark-cloth couches that make your bare legs sweat and itch in the summer—a '70s cowboys-and-Indians print, with arms made out of wood.

"I don't know why I remember that stuff," she said, almost apologizing. I told her remembering made sense to me. Ivan

Ilych, Tolstoy's dying protagonist, turns his face to the back of a couch so that he can stare at a button. Zooming in makes an unbearable world feel small enough to manage.

Six years ago, we needed to board a rickety plane owned by the second-most-deadly airline in the world. Hurricane warnings were all over the news that day, and train tracks were being washed away by floods. We couldn't wait the storm out—we had to fly to pick up the son we were adopting, but I could barely move my legs to walk up the ramp, they were shaking so badly.

We made our ascent through black skies, and I thought the turbulence would shake my teeth out of their sockets. As we broke through the worst of the clouds, the seams of the plane gasped and creaked, and out the window, everything below was a sea of purple for miles and miles and miles. Sunlight falling on those clouds was otherworldly, a sick, pale, iridescent yellow. The storm was made of mammoth Fibonacci twists—inky indigos bloodied by red-plum stains, foamy amethysts, dirty billows ignited by flashes of internal fire.

This was Prospero's brew from *The Tempest*, and I knew I was going to die. My whole body went weak. I thought that I should pray, but all I could do was whisper, "Save us," and then count slowly: 1, 2, 3, 4, 5, 6, 7, 8, 9, 10 . . . forward and backward, pinching my second finger and thumb together in a pulse. Sometimes you freeze and count to ten, or you stare at a button, or you hide behind the couch and trace the lines of the upholstery.

My friend said, "Yes. That's what it's like. That's exactly it."

She took a deep breath and walked me inside the home where he had hurt her. Time had worn it down, turned it so fragile that even our breath seemed to make the walls of her memories shudder. As she shut the door behind us, I saw her hand flutter, searching for something. It landed on a light switch, and she flipped it on as if she were pulling the pin of a grenade. A dud. No electricity. We'd have to make our way in the dark. I hit my iPhone flashlight, and she grabbed my arm so I could follow her.

"Here's the kitchen," she said. As she yanked a ratty curtain to the side, a window over the sink let in a wash of gray light. She pulled the refrigerator door open. No food inside, no hum of current. A dead fly. We breathed in air that had been trapped inside a metal box for two decades.

The sink was ringed with a brown line. Her mom and dad had yelled at each other in that room, severe words that turned like dirty water caught in an eternal drain, flying round and round but never leaving the room.

Down the hall was the bathroom where my friend used to cry in the shower until she puked. She ran her hands over the hot and cold taps, cranking them until they made dry heaves. Cave crickets launched themselves like men from cannons, blasting their little brains against the cold ceramic.

She told me she was nine here once, making a naked ball of herself while the water hit her back in needles. She told me how she rocked back and forth on her toes and sucked the tears off her own knees until she made four purple marks.

The water tasted like salt and Irish Spring soap, and she wanted to stay behind that locked door forever.

We walked down steps into the crude basement where words shot like bullets. These shelves had once held canning jars full of skinless peaches and blanched tomatoes. Now there were just four half-empty gallons of white paint with their lids rusted shut. They sat at the base of the wall where he had held her by the throat.

Back up the staircase, we climbed against the creak and groan of that old place. She showed me the closet where she went to hide—a sweet darkness where she learned to make herself invisible. "It would have been easier if I hadn't loved them," she said, "but children kiss the hand that strikes them."

"Show me where you prayed for Jesus to stop it," I asked. She took me to the living room, and we both knelt down in that spot. I prayed for her there, and I cried for her pain. Here we talked to God straight without cutting any corners or making any excuses.

My God, my God, why did you forsake her?
> Why were you so far from saving her,
> so far from her cries of anguish?
My God, she cried out by day, but you did not answer,
> by night, but she found no rest.

ADAPTED FROM PSALM 22:1-2, NIV

We didn't force an answer; we just talked to the Lord. Then, when we were finished, we left the house behind us. The front door wouldn't shut easily, so we slammed it until the frame shuddered.

Outside in the sun, we sat on the grass and watched a northern harrier stretch his wings against the summer currents, sailing like a ship on good seas. We'd been breathing shallow, so we leaned back and inhaled deeply, sizing that house up from the outside while the August heat made the oil on our faces shine.

Speaking Pain Out Loud

When I was in my midthirties, friends began telling me stories of long-term abuse that they had suffered as children. Fathers, uncles, and fellow church members were the perpetrators—adults who should have been trustworthy. I had studied the origin of evil in theology classes, but these first-person accounts made my old conclusions feel shallow and evasive. It's one thing to sit in a classroom and talk about atrocities done to strangers; it's another to listen while a good friend tells you that she was seven when she begged Jesus to make the rapes stop—a prayer that wasn't answered for a decade, when she finally left home for good.

Sickness and death are hard enough wounds to process in faith, but child abuse is even more difficult. Because I was a young mother when I heard these stories, I knew what it meant to protect a child, so I couldn't understand how any parent—especially a divine Father—could stand by while a little one was being wounded. I'd rip somebody's face off if he tried to hurt my baby. How could anyone just sit and watch? As the ugly reality of abuse grew inside me, I found it increasingly difficult to trust a God who had the ability to stop pain but who chose to wait instead.

So I began to work back through theories of evil with my heart instead of just my mind. Some of the ideas I read only made me angrier. Now that I had a personal context for suffering, I couldn't give credence to scholars who addressed sorrow with cold mathematics. Bedside manner matters in a theologian just as much as it does in a doctor, and posture tends to reveal as much about a scholar as his arguments.

The worst theories reminded me of that proud oncologist who walked into the exam room when one of my grandfathers was suffering from cancer. "He's going to die an excruciating death," that doctor said, "and there's nothing I can do about it." It was a cruel thing for a physician to say, but I've seen theologians adopt a similar attitude when dealing with the agony of a broken world. "Sin broke everything. People hurt people. It is what it is."

There's no way around it—some truths of the Bible are difficult to hear. But if there is no compassion when communicating the theology of suffering—if there is only systematic, Vulcan resolve—that scholar doesn't reflect the heart of Christ, no matter what information has been crammed into his head. Even when God is severe, he does not project indifference.

Finally, I stumbled into *A Grief Observed*, a book C. S. Lewis wrote after his wife died. Here was the horrified roar

I needed. As I read about Lewis's suffering, I realized that he wasn't just offering the cerebral facts of his theology but his emotional vulnerability; here was a real human speaking as a lonely husband still reeling from sorrow. What Lewis didn't write was as important to me as what he did. He didn't recite platitudes like "God works in mysterious ways!" or "Rejoice in all things!" He didn't hold doctrine up like a Hula-Hoop for a little dog to jump through. He wrote in the spirit of David in Psalm 22:

> My God, my God, why have you forsaken me?
>> Why are you so far from saving me,
>> so far from my cries of anguish?
> My God, I cry out by day, but you do not answer,
>> by night, but I find no rest.
>
> VERSES 1-2, NIV

In this psalm, we find a believer who didn't make excuses for a distant God. Instead, he cried out, expecting the Lord to engage, pouring out the whole awful story of how it felt to suffer. David even went so far as to accuse God of doing something that the Lord would never do: forsaking one of his children.

The psalmist didn't try to pretend like the silence of God was sweet. He wailed in his lonely devastation, trusting the Lord enough to be vulnerable with him instead of trying to pass off the dishonest lingo of faked religious submission. If this sort of confrontation doesn't feel like trust to you, remember that we tend to hide our real selves from people we don't love; only our oldest, dearest friends usually get the full scoop. God got the full scoop from David, and he got the full scoop from C. S. Lewis.

In his sermon series on praying through the emotions, Tim Keller warned us against "nicely manicured and managed little theologically correct confessional prayers." Instead, he said that our engagement with God should express our feelings "pre-reflectively."[1] This means that before we try to figure everything out, we should run to our Father and pour our hearts out to him. This also means it's okay if what we need to say to him is messy. According to Keller, both religious and secular viewpoints can adopt unhealthy, extreme stances about feelings. The religious try to deny strong emotions while the secular world uses feelings to validate behavior. The mature believer, however, walks a middle road of vivid expression lived out in a context of trust and obedience.

David's psalms show us how healthy it is to take our feelings to the Lord, who loves us enough to engage with who we really are. I used to try to shield God from my frustrations with him, but I don't do that as much anymore. Now when I am hurting, or after I sit with friends who are traumatized, I take every detail directly to the Lord who hasn't intervened. Instead of lying to God about how much I trust him (if I don't), praying forced prayers (that I don't really mean), and trying to pull the wool over God's eyes and my own, I bring my doubt, weakness, and sorrow straight to my Maker and let him be the Father he is.

My God, my God, you shut the mouths of lions, stilled
a storm on the sea, and healed the blind. But you
didn't help my friend. I know you are good. I know
you will dry every tear. But you had the ability to stop
the abuse of a child—a child who cried to you for
help!—and you held back. Where were you? Why did
you forsake her? I can't even sleep at night, thinking
about it.

Even as I am pouring out my pain to the Lord, I know
that he always has the authority and the power to respond
to my suffering as he responded to Job's. Job was devastated
by losing all his kids, his money, his health, and the respect
of his wife—far more of a loss than Lewis or David ever
faced—yet God was still verbally severe with him: "Brace
yourself like a man; I will question you, and you shall answer
me. Where were you when I laid the earth's foundation?"[2] On
and on those chapters go, rising into a holy crescendo. They
are terrifying, relentless, and wonderful, some of my favorite chapters in the whole Bible. But while the roar of God's
response to Job shows me the rights of my sovereign ruler, the
story of Lazarus shows me a God who chose to weep beside
the tomb of a friend. Unapologetically, the Bible offers both
sides of our complex Lord.

Have you ever noticed how differently grief works through
Lazarus's two sisters, Mary and Martha? After saying, "Lord,
if you had been here, my brother would not have died,"
type A Martha managed to say the right religious words:

"But even now I know that God will give you whatever you ask of him."[3]

Mary didn't get that far; instead, she blubbered out the same phrase Martha spoke—a phrase their whole family had probably been whispering in sickrooms for days—the sort of phrase that becomes a chorus when you are hoping against hope for a loved one. "Lord, if you had been here, my brother would not have died," Mary said to Jesus.[4] Hadn't she and Martha used this thought to comfort one another while waiting for the Savior to arrive? "When Jesus gets here, it will all be okay. Jesus won't let him die. Hold out, Mary. Hold out, Martha. Jesus will come."

Then future tense became past perfect tense. "He will be here" was suddenly "If you had been here . . ." and Mary cried honestly before the Christ, who was too late.

How did Jesus respond in the presence of her raw grief? John said, "When Jesus saw her weeping, and the Jews who had come with her also weeping, he was deeply moved in his spirit and greatly troubled."[5] Then, even though resurrection was imminent, the Messiah sat down to weep with a friend who was weeping.

Had Job not complained honestly to the Lord, he might have missed the most stunning poetic defense of all time. Had Mary not complained honestly to the Lord, she might have missed a chance to learn about her Maker's compassion. Both walked away richer because they were vulnerable with a God who could take it.

The God Who Didn't

My questions about the kindness of God became personal when our daughter was born with a heart defect. I'm embarrassed to tell you about this because I've seen friends face more excruciating circumstances with much greater strength, but a hole in my baby's septum was all it took to crush me. In the wake of this news, I spent more than a thousand nights appealing to God, kneeling beside my daughter's bed while she was sleeping. I would put my hand on her chest, feeling her little heart beat three inches from my palm, growing increasingly frustrated with her Creator.

Why would he spin the rings of Saturn and not bother to fix a nickel-sized flaw inside my child? Involuntarily, I'd reach one hand up in the pitch dark, thinking about the red storms of Jupiter, trying not to ask him why he was more interested in the "wow" factor than in the health of my precious child. Did he want praise from the masses instead of one desperate mother's gratitude? Accusations bubbled secretly inside my soul, but I tried not to feel them. I was determined to keep a right attitude, in part because I didn't understand the magnitude of the gospel. I was still trying to earn God's blessings by proving my faith to him. I thought that if I could prop my belief up during this trial, keeping my trust in perfect submission, God might reward me by healing my daughter.

Each time we went in for checkups, every muscle in my back tensed up as I waited for news that the miracle I wanted (and had earned?) had been performed. In a dark room, while a stranger pressed a sonogram wand into my baby's soft, pink body, my eyes fixated on the cardiac monitor. The blood flow sloshed in red and blue pixels, but the motion was all wrong. I could see the leak. The defect hadn't been healed; in fact, her heart was enlarging. I felt fear and fury rise in my chest. *Why not, God? What is your deal?* But I pushed that anger down. I pushed it away.

When my daughter was six years old, doctors told us it was time for surgery. As we stood with her in the prep room, every maternal impulse screamed that I should stay beside her, but as the anesthesia took over her tiny body, my husband put his arm around me, and he walked me into the lobby. I had been as brave as all mothers are in such circumstances, smiling and kissing her while those pretty eyes fluttered to sleep, but the sight of my daughter breathing through a mask, then passing into a drug-induced stupor, had been too much for me to bear. In the waiting room, I slumped forward in a metal chair without my baby, feeling utterly helpless before a God who hadn't given me the most important thing I had ever asked him to do.

George Orwell's book *1984* details the torture of rebellious humans—torture that persists until citizens are finally forced to "love" Big Brother. Beneath my paralytic fear, I felt a similar sort of entrapment. Did I really have the freedom to embrace or reject him? He held all the power. What kind of love could I give someone who left me no other option but devotion? This thought felt terrifyingly rebellious, and it shamed me as it flickered around in my consciousness. I didn't want God to see what I was tempted to believe.

Unfortunately, I didn't respond to my doubt as David responded to his. I didn't trust God enough to get real with him. Instead, I tried to hide my naked resentment. I was like Adam and Eve, holding up ridiculous handfuls of fig leaves, thinking I could prevent God from seeing the truth about my feelings. I held my faith as I held my breath—but how long can a person hold either of those? We're only mortals, after all.

The Language of the Wounded

After walking through the squeeze of those years, it makes more sense to me when those who have suffered emerge from trauma asking, "If God is all-powerful—if he's all-good—why didn't he keep me safe?" Long-term grief can help us understand why single friends are angry after years of being told that they would be given a godly spouse if they would just trust the Lord and stay sexually pure. It can show us why their hearts break after agonizing, lonely years of online dating. It can show us why they want to scream at other people's baby showers, and why they threaten to give up, and why they threaten to rebel. It can show us why they wonder if God sees them at all.

Long-term pain can show us why the guy who just lost his third job and his wife of twenty years feels too ashamed and too angry to show up at church on Sunday morning. Sure, he shouldn't have punched a hole in the drywall in his garage, but we also know why he did it. Once we have suffered, we can imagine the unbearable pressure this man feels to keep smiling in public because "weak" men can't start over. We know why he's scared that God won't catch him because life so far has been pretty darn hard.

Technically, of course, our suffering shouldn't be a surprise. God's Word tells us that life on planet Earth is going to hurt, but a warning can't always prepare us for the jolt of real pain. Until we've *known* deep, long agony, we might not wonder how the Lord's promises to care for our needs reconcile with the hard facts. When suffering gets real, the seams of our faith groan under the strain. We find out how hard it is to come home to an empty house night after night. We find out how brutal it is to survive divorce. We wake up another morning choking in the wake of betrayal. We fall in bed exhausted after a day of humiliating failure. We limp after abuse. We shudder in the throes of disease. The hours and days of such experiences stir up questions we don't want to ask.

When health, wealth, and prosperity teachers promise that God wants us all to be happy, they speak in direct contradiction to thousands of lives of faithful men and women who have lived in long and profound difficulty. They also ignore the confession of the apostle Paul, a believer who was allowed to grow so discouraged during one point of his ministry that he despaired even of life.[6] Whatever God meant by providing for our needs has to allow room for all of this.

On Facebook and Instagram, I regularly see Christians using the hashtag #blessed to celebrate a caramel latte or a beach vacation. I don't doubt God's generosity in the little things, but I do have trouble knowing how to process these blessings when another friend sits in a hospital room, tending a child whose body weakens under a critical prognosis. Extravagant, beautiful things happen on planet Earth, but terrible, unbearable things do too.

When I am hurting deeply, formal theological explanations of suffering never seem to calm my restless soul because long-term pain isn't something that logic alone can fix. If the Lord is going to allow the world to be this brutal, I need more than the math of things. I need to know that my Father feels pain intensely as I do and that his love for me will prove stronger than any single moment of weakness that suffering evokes. I need to be free to cry out to him, knowing that he sees me and that he cares.

Those Who Cannot Keep Themselves Alive

If God detests the frantic outcry of the broken, I don't know why he would have allowed Psalm 22 to remain in the Bible or why Jesus would have quoted it. Instead, the Lord seems to be showing us that the passion of human grief doesn't shock him. In fact, by citing Psalm 22 on the cross, I think Jesus is showing us how he took all human abuse into his own flesh. *Jesus says the words we say because he felt the pain we feel.* He not only hurt for us but also as us. Then, as he shuddered as one abused, he pointed us along the rails of Psalm 22 to the fulfillment of all suffering.

> All the rich of the earth will feast and worship;
>> all who go down to the dust will kneel before him—
>> those who cannot keep themselves alive.[7]

"Those who cannot keep themselves alive." I need those six words desperately because they describe me. Don't they describe you? We cannot keep ourselves alive when we sit in hospital chairs, unable to breathe, waiting for news from the surgeon. We cannot keep ourselves alive when we grieve beside the unbelief of our children. We cannot keep ourselves alive when we are subject to injustice, to abuse, to pain, and to murder. We cannot keep ourselves alive when we are lonely, ashamed, scared. We cannot keep ourselves alive when those who should shield us ravage us instead.

We know what it means to give up the ghost of our strength at the hands of overwhelming odds, and that is a terrifying feeling—but David tells us that one day we dead and dying will rise and feast. Maybe today we can't choke down a crappy cup of waiting-room coffee because the earth's grip has tightened around our throats, but a time will come for us to celebrate because the Jesus who died for us—the same Jesus who also cried out, "My God, why have you forsaken me?"—knows and provides for our limits.

One of my favorite old Christian myths has origins that predate Christianity. It's the story of a mother pelican who faces a time of famine, but rather than watch her children starve, she wounds her body, feeding her babies with her own flesh and blood. In times of intense suffering, I have gone back to that image over and again, reminding myself that this is the sort of God I am accusing of indifference. My pain might temporarily blind me to his pain, but here is a God who willingly entered the drought lands to harm himself so that we might live. When I accuse him of being distant, of not caring, of not feeling, I am not seeing what he has truly done for and with me. When I feed off my God, I feed off his own agony, willingly offered.

As my daughter was waiting for her heart surgery, well-meaning religious people said the oddest things to me. Some told me that if we prayed "the right way," Jesus would heal her. Some told me that God allowed my baby's heart to be damaged because of our sin, so I needed to confess things I couldn't remember doing. These comments made me feel rebuked, isolated, angry, and lonely. My daughter was in danger, and I didn't have the strength to maintain a performance for God.

I didn't need a locker-room pep talk, and I didn't need threats. My suffering wasn't a reality show with a cash reward at the end of the season. I needed to be reminded that my God suffered with me and that he was real, close, and big enough to carry me through the darkness of all my doubts and fears, no matter how weak I was at any given moment. For years, Christian leaders told me to put my faith in the facts and my feelings would follow, but they didn't tell me that God would still carry me even when my emotions were stronger than my faith. I have been so relieved to find an engaged God at the end of myself, a Savior who upholds me, instead of a wooden idol who constantly needs to be kept from toppling over.

If you are walking with long-term sorrow, if you fear the strength of the pain you've pushed down and out of sight, I think it's okay to cry out, "My God, my God! Where have you been? If you had been here, I wouldn't have died!" When that question is rolling around inside you, God knows it's there. You don't fool him by trying to repress it, and you're not going to shock him by admitting what you feel. Trusting him means trusting him with your whole self.

He knows when you are mad, scared, damaged, tied in a knot. He knows when you need to walk back through the house of your trauma and name the nightmares room by room. If you've been carrying a painful load forever, it's probably going to be tough to learn this sort of vulnerability. Especially if you have spent most of your life trying to be strong, trying to hold everything together for everybody, learning to rely upon a God who doesn't need you to be the load-bearing agent may be slow going. But as you go through the process of exchanging a yoke that is heavy for a yoke that is light,[8] you're going to find a God who can handle the real you, no matter how messed up pain has left you. Not all friendships can stomach this level of authenticity, but your friendship with Jesus can.

The Lord might not coddle you, of course. Instead, he might roar to restore your withering heart as he roared at Job.

He might throw the curtain back on idols that you need to smash. He might expose unhealthy demands that you need to let go. More often than not, however, his approach seems to be gentle—especially with the long-suffering, for he is a shield about the grieving, the lifter of their heads.[9] A broken and contrite heart, he does not despise.[10] He gives grace to the humble.[11] "A bruised reed he will not break, and a faintly burning wick he will not quench."[12] This is the Physician we approach, and while we cannot know which surgery he will perform until we approach him in truth, what we can know is that he will operate in love and that his care will do us good.

In 1961, a Soviet doctor named Leonid Rogozov found himself stranded in Antarctica with appendicitis. To survive, he had to perform his own appendectomy. It was a horrific, nearly two-hour ordeal, performed without gloves and mostly by feeling around in his own abdomen, since mirrors confused him. Every five minutes, he took breaks because the pain and nausea were so intense.[13] I can't imagine attempting such a thing, and yet, every time I read Rogozov's story, I think about how many Christians are trying to become more Christlike by straining to repair their own insides. No surgeon would choose self-surgery if another option were available—and yet Christians make this very choice every single day.

God never meant for the Christian life to be one bright day of salvation followed by four decades of pulling ourselves up by our bootstraps, trying harder to be better. In fact, in his letter to the Galatians, Paul sharply confronted Christians who were trying to heal themselves by saying, "Are you so foolish? Having begun by the Spirit, are you now being perfected by the flesh?"[14] By saying this, Paul wasn't being cruel. He was trying to shock hurting people awake—people who would eventually self-destruct if they kept trying to manage healing on their own. "Apart from me you can do nothing," Jesus said[15]—and that includes healing from long-term pain.

So go to him in honest despair like David. Go in honest disappointment like Mary. Go in anger. Go in shame. Go in doubt. Tell him those words that repeat over and over again inside your mind. If you're scared to go, hold your breath if you need to; count to ten; walk shaking. But slowly begin to rest the impossible burden that is weighing you down at his feet. This won't be the end of your complex journey with suffering, of course, but it is the right beginning.

Protein Soup: A Letter to Those Living in Chaos

I live with a vestibular disorder that causes bouts of vertigo. This isn't merry-go-round dizziness; it's like falling off a cliff into 360 degrees of rotation. Usually, it hits first thing in the morning, which means that I open my eyes in a familiar room and then grab the sides of my bed as the whole world revolves. Sitting up makes me vomit. When I lie still, the windows spin. I can't even walk to the bathroom when it's bad—either my husband has to guide me, or I have to crawl on the floor, feeling with my hands for direction. When I'm lucky, it's over in twenty-four hours. Once, it lasted a week.

The first time this happened, I felt more vulnerable than I have ever felt in my life. Within seconds, all my bearings disappeared. I didn't know what was happening to me, and I couldn't think rationally to figure it out. A stroke? An embolism? I cried out for my husband, holding his arm up against my face while whimpering, "I think I'm dying. Please don't leave me. Please don't even move." It was that fast. All my ferocity and wit were gone in a snap, and I was reduced to a sniffling heap of fear.

If you've experienced sudden emotional trauma, you know how it operates like vertigo in the soul. The phone rings with terrible news, or we stumble into a text message we were never meant to see, and within five seconds—within five words—everything that's familiar in our world contorts. A life that was normal and predictable yesterday looks so strange now, and we know that it will look strange from here on out.

The Weakness Chaos Reveals

I wish I were one of those poised, unshakable women I've read about in novels—maybe an Elinor Dashwood, who handles even the worst news with brave composure. In reality, however, my track record with chaos isn't so great. Instead of keeping my voice calm, I've wailed in horror. Instead of staying firm and quiet, I've lashed about in confused reactivity.

More than a decade ago, someone I trusted made a selfish and dishonest choice. A lot of people, including my own husband and kids, were hurt deeply by his behavior, but instead of owning his mistake, this person dug in his heels and said that God had told him to do what he had done.

In shock and in anger, I fired off a pointed message, telling that man exactly what I thought of him and his actions. A lot of what I wrote was true, but e-mail is almost always the wrong way to handle intense frustration. For so many reasons, it would have been wiser for me to confront the man directly. Instead of writing me back, this man made copies of my private message and spread them in our community. I wasn't given a chance to explain the context of my words, so playing the victim angle, he collected a whole team of men to rebuke me.

I was stunned that our conflict had come to all this. Of course, I was ashamed that my fervor had been exposed to the public eye, but my heart was even more broken to realize that someone I had once trusted wasn't trustworthy. It felt as if the world were spinning, that right and wrong had switched places, and that justice would never come. In the crazy aftermath of this mess, I promised myself that I would never respond in fury again. No matter what. No matter how cruelly or dishonestly anyone behaved, no matter how hurt I was, I would trust God and wait for his rescue.

Then I got a second chance. Several years later, a similar situation arose. This time, the consequences were even more severe, but I remembered my promise. I waited quietly three days, then a week, then two weeks. Honestly, I felt a little proud of how much I had grown in my faith.

Since I was "doing suffering right this time," I expected the Lord to rush in and patch things up while I held myself in meek submission. However, that's not what happened.

Instead, he let the consequences pile up heavier and higher until I began to feel trapped and hopeless.

"When are you going to stop this, Lord? When are you going to show them who's boss?" I prayed. Nothing. Total silence from the heavens. At last, the pressure grew too great, and I flew into a flurry of angry text messages, stabbing and slashing like Peter in the garden of Gethsemane. Fear and anger commandeered my willpower, and as the dust settled, I had to admit that I didn't even have the fortitude to keep my own best promises to myself.

This was a tough realization. I had wanted to be an icon. Instead, I was a grown-up child throwing a fit. As much as I wanted to be like that old Amy Carmichael quote—"A cup *brimful of sweet water* cannot spill even one drop of bitter water, however suddenly jolted"[1]—that person wasn't me. Unshakable faith sounded great in theory, but in real life, I was kind of a brat.

Rich Mullins once wrote that we are "awfully small / And not as strong as we think we are,"[2] but most of the time, I don't feel small. I am a firstborn child, a type A, driven doer who refuses to back down. When the going gets tough, I roll up my sleeves and work harder. Only in trauma have I come to find out how frail I truly am. Only in chaos does the illusion of my own power dissolve.

In one of my favorite old devotional books, *31 Days of Praise*, Ruth Myers thanked God for difficult people.[3] Her prayer always makes me cringe because I'd rather pray fire (and rats, and crickets, and snakes) down on my enemies' heads. Still, I must admit that God regularly uses "bad guys" to expose my stubborn and hidden sins. Times of shock, injustice, and even danger suck the hidden infections out of my heart and throw them into the daylight. This process is embarrassing, maddening, and grossly unfair at times—but also, it's surgery. Sometimes the growth that we need the most can't be accomplished in dignity, safety, or privacy.

When my dad had his first heart operation, there were signs hanging in the hospital hallways, asking visitors not to look into patient rooms as they passed. I'd never stayed in a hospital long enough to consider that point of courtesy before, but as I sat in a recovery room with Dad, the request began to make more sense. When you've had yourself sawed open and sewn back together, when even breathing hurts, you don't want to feel as if you're on display.

The same is true of emotional trauma. If you're facing chaos right now, you probably wish you had a magical "don't look" sign to hang on the front door of your life. Yet we live in the age of the Internet, where everybody sees everything all the time.

An ex-wife is checking Facebook when she sees a picture her ex-husband has posted—it's "the other woman" with him in a hot tub. Their teenage sons are on Facebook, and she's taught them to be moral all their lives. Now their middle-aged dad has gone off the deep end. How are those boys supposed to process this?

Or an adult daughter flaunts her rebellion on Twitter, and pain intense enough to break her parents' hearts flashes before hundreds of family members and friends. They love her. They would welcome her home any minute, forgiving everything she's ever done. The public shame of the situation means nothing to them compared to their ache for her soul. And yet they still must figure out how to respond when people at work or church ask them how she's doing. They want to scream, "You're on her Twitter! You *see* how she's doing! We'd rather die than live through this!" Every inquiry is a sword that runs straight through their bodies at random moments in the week. Her parents can barely breathe as they try to keep their composure.

All the mess is out there all the time, and it's increasingly hard to decide what to ignore and what to address. How do you juggle questions that feel a little like concern and a lot like nosiness? How do you find the courage to live any sort of regular life in this kind of chaos?

Most of us just limp along in pain, trying to imitate normalcy in the wake of devastation. But then there's the morning when it's finally just too much, the camel's back breaks, and we make emotional fools of ourselves. You know the T-shirt that says, "I'm sorry for what I said when I was hungry"? There should be a shirt like that for people surviving trauma. "I'm sorry for what I said when my life was falling apart."

Faith, Work, Relationships

People in chaos often experience a hit in three big areas: faith, work, and relationships. Depending on the situation, these blows may fall in a different order, but still, knowing some general categories of potential fallout can help you feel less weird and less alone if such troubles come to you. When I was living through chaos, I wasn't prepared for the impact of tension on so many different parts of life. It would have helped for someone to tell me that certain stress reactions are normal—not to justify those reactions, but to help me know that there's a way out when the whole building of your life feels as if it's collapsing on top of you.

Impact on Faith

If you are walking through chaos right now, your relationship with God may feel as if it's taken a hit. You might find yourself asking questions about the Lord that bother you—questions that make you feel lonely or even guilty.

For example, I couldn't forgive the people who had hurt me for a long, long time. I knew that unforgiveness was wrong, so I kept trying to forgive and forget. But every morning I would wake up to realize that I hadn't done either. No matter what my theology told me to do, no matter how fiercely I decided to willfully let it go "once and for all," the anger wouldn't go away. It was hard for me to talk about this internal struggle because I was afraid most friends would give me flippant advice like "Don't let bitterness overtake your life!" or "Unforgiveness is the grave we dig ourselves." But forgiving wasn't that simple. (Wouldn't I have already let it go if I could?) Because the wound was so deep, learning to rest active pain in the sovereignty of the Lord was like learning to walk after a traumatic accident. Rehabilitation was slow and grueling, and I couldn't make it happen all at once. My faith muscles were torn and damaged, and I needed months of spiritual therapy sessions with Jesus and his gospel before I could run. Even now, I limp sometimes when I'm tired.

If the chaos in your life is financial, physical, or medical, it's also normal for your "peace that passes understanding" circuit to get a short in it. Sure, for a few minutes in the morning, you might be able to trust God, but by evening, you panic and berate yourself for your doubt. It seems as if a child of God would handle uncertainty better than this, but trauma has shown you that you're weaker than you realized, and you hate what you see in yourself.

Impact on Work

Chaos can also impact your performance at work. "You missed line four in the inventory!" your manager screeches, as if he's found the holy grail. He's "that guy" at the office, the one who gets an ego rush from catching other people's mistakes. He hasn't been this happy about anything since he stepped on a baby duck during the petting farm field trip in the fourth grade.

His pedantry makes you nervous, and as you feel him breathing down your neck, you start to make more mistakes than you normally would. He senses fear and ramps up his surveillance. You daydream about quitting, but you can't, so you take a few more steps and fail again. Every time you hear his footsteps in the hall, you cringe.

Once I received life-altering news two weeks before I was supposed to start a new teaching job. The material I was supposed to cover in class was complex, requiring hours of study; and I needed vivacity and humor to keep rooms full of teenagers engaged. Even in the best of circumstances, I would have struggled to perform this task, but I didn't get the best circumstances. I got trauma. Most details of that first year are blurry now—but I will always remember who was gracious with me and who was severe. Simply surviving those months was a monumental feat—mostly because it took every ounce of faith and courage I had to keep getting back on the horse after falling off.

Impact on Relationships

In such circumstances, work leaves you so drained that you show up for marriage, friendship, and parenting with a headache. You love these people more than anybody in the world, so you determine to be okay for their sake. You smile. You make dinner. You light the candles. You send a text message. But chaos seeps in through the cracks, under every window and door, into all your dirty rooms, into your laundry piles, and into those hectic meals when you never stop to look anybody in the eyes.

Finally you collapse in bed and cry because time is passing and you've goofed it all up. You'll never get these days back again—days you needed to be there for them, but you were so empty that you had nothing left to give the people who mattered most to you. Everything is a mess. Everything.

If that's your life, I get it. If you could read some of the words I wrote in anger, if you could see me sitting on my kitchen floor crying till I nearly puked, if you could hear me yelling into the woods behind my house, you wouldn't feel even a little bit embarrassed to show me how broken you are right now. More than once, I wept in my van in the dark, trying to pray. I made stupid mistakes at work. I didn't give my family some things I wish I had been able to give them. Chaos is just so devastatingly hard.

Yet, as someone who has survived a season like this, I want to tell you that you're at an important crossroads. The desperation you feel right now is not wasted, and the mistakes you are making aren't wasted either. In fact, in some weird way, you're standing at a portal, on the brink of some of the most important wisdom of your whole life. Yes, you're being vivisected, but trauma is more than an instrument of torture. After chaos breaks you down, God can use it to teach you to fly.

Protein Soup

When I was a child, I lived in an old farmhouse in rural Kentucky. Houses there can be miles apart, so almost everybody has a security light. Sometimes these lights are mounted on tall wooden poles, and other times they are mounted near the gutters on a roof corner. When we took trips down the Bluegrass Parkway at night, I'd lean my head over against the window so I could feel the vibrations of the road in my skull bones, and I'd fall into a sort of a dreamlike state, watching miles of black fields flutter by in the shadows.

In the distance, those security lights blasted against the darkness, making me imagine a visitation from the heavenly host, orbs of glory between acres of corn, cattle, and hay. Some bulbs cast an industrial, ice-blue glow while others glittered gold. When I was five or six, I decided the difference was a code. Families with the warmer lights were generous— homes with little old ladies who grew African violets and little old men who carried packs of Juicy Fruit gum in their pockets. Homes with colder lights harbored spinsters, skin- flints, and murderers. We had a security light near the corner of my room, but I never could tell which color it was because up close, they all seem the same.

I began collecting insects in 1980, and nights that summer I'd stand beneath the buzz of our own halogen moon, holding a butterfly net that I had made from an old broomstick, a coat hanger, and a thin pillowcase. Tiny gray moths were cheap and plentiful, tossing in a mad, silent fury. If you kept your mouth open, you'd suck one in and have to cough it back up. Sometimes, you'd inhale one up your nose. There were hard, black beetles, too, slapping and knocking into things like nine-year-old boys killing time in a whatnot shop. When you start to study insects, you only see these swarms, but after a few nights of standing out there, your eyes adjust, and you realize what you are looking for and what you aren't.

On the far edge of the light circle, a luna moth spread her wings in the grass. She was perfect, newly awakened from pupation. Kids usually find luna moths dead—maybe a single wing torn off by a bird, or a whole broken body battered in the front grille of a car. But a perfect new luna, sitting alone in the dark, will make you hold your breath. God made fancier moths but none more ethereal. Lunas are like sea glass or frost on the first two weeks of a garden. They are like Rivendell and powdered sugar. Their wing tails cross at the ends like lace-trimmed sock ankles on a tiny girl sitting still on Sunday morning. And when a new luna moves, she moves with the control of a ballet dancer at the barre.

Not too many weeks before, this same moth was a fat, crawling larva. Then, heavy with her own mass, she lumbered up some branch until she found a spot to attach herself and spin a cocoon. Inside that cocoon, every piece of her old body liquefied into a soup of her own proteins. While she waited, she was formless. When I first found out how all that happened, I wondered if it was frightening to feel yourself breaking down. I mean, imagine your arms, your legs, your fingers, your everything turning into a big pile of goo. Does God whisper something like hope to all the wee little insects settling down into their own undoing? Do they know that they will soon come together again? Does metamorphosis feel normal as an itch on the end of your nose, or does it feel like the end of the world?

Schools teach kids about the life cycles of insects by coloring pages or by videos, summing up the whole shebang with labels like "egg, larva, pupa, adult." When you name a miracle by steps, it feels cut-and-dried, but when you raise insects yourself, and when you spend slow time examining them, you begin to see a thousand nuances of growth, in-between stages that make up larger stages. You learn what must go right, not four times but five hundred times, before a moth can emerge to stretch new frosted wings under a security light. A different sort of respect develops when you get that close up.

Something similar happens when we get a close-up view of chaos. We begin to realize that big stages like "before cancer" and "after cancer" break down into specific days and hours that require miracles to survive. At social-media distance we might hear that someone "got divorced," but at the distance of a text or a phone call, we hear that a friend cried her guts out on the day that she divided the wedding towels, the spatulas, and the pets.

Once, I cut open a cocoon to see what was inside, and I thought I would find a solid little moth body forming. Instead, I found a stew of nothing that seemed as if it had never been anything definite and could never be anything definite again. If it were possible to cut open a human soul during chaos, I think maybe this is what we would look like too. A casual observer staring into our mess couldn't believe that we had ever been okay or that we would ever be okay again.

If I Fall, Can You Catch Me?

I was the cynical, nerd kid at church camp who wouldn't do the trust fall. While all the other teenagers were climbing up bleachers and plunging backward into the arms of their fellow campers, I was trying to guess their median ACT scores and estimating how many pounds of pressure those scrawny arms could handle. I thought about the risk of spinal injury and paralysis before deciding that I didn't need a bunch of sweaty teenagers to teach me about reliance—I could learn that myself, thanks.

I still think trust falls are goofy, but cynicism gets serious when I apply a deep posture of suspicion to my willingness to trust the grace of Jesus, making it impossible for me to lean upon him. "What if he doesn't catch me? What if my sin is too heavy? What if he's just a cosmic, snarling pedant who enjoys pointing out every line in the inventory I missed?" Sadly, I tend to trust myself more than I trust anybody, so self-reliance feels a lot safer than a free fall into faith. Only when chaos gets so intense that I can no longer manage my own world do I find out how big God's love and strength actually are.

Facing a situation that exposed the depth of his vulnerability, the apostle Paul said, "Three times I pleaded with the Lord to take it away from me." But God didn't take that situation away. Instead, God said, "My grace is sufficient for you, for my power is made perfect in weakness."[4]

I'm sure that hearing *no* was tough for Paul. Wouldn't most of us expect something more from a God who had taken the trouble to blind somebody in the middle of a road to get his attention? After that big "Shazam!" why wouldn't God give Paul skills he legitimately needed to ace Christianity?

But the *no* here was more important than a *yes* ever could have been. The shock of a refusal forced Paul to not only accept his inabilities but also to revel in them. A *no* is what finally gave Paul enough failure to say, "Therefore I will boast all the more gladly about my weaknesses, so that Christ's power may rest on me. That is why, for Christ's sake, I delight in weaknesses, in insults, in hardships, in persecutions, in difficulties. For when I am weak, then I am strong."[5]

Over and over again, the New Testament tries to tell us something we have so much trouble hearing: that the goal of Christianity is dependent union—an unusual sort of God-human relationship that doesn't have a true parallel in the human-to-human world. God uses earthly metaphors to hint at what he means by this bond—sometimes bride-groom language or parent-child comparisons. But no human relationship can catch all of what's happening in our unity with God because he is more intimate with us than anything we will ever share with another person.

If you read back through the New Testament, you will notice that the Bible uses strange phrases like "Christ in you" to describe this intimate union. Sometimes we are called a "dwelling place," and other times we are called branches on a vine. This isn't like anything we read about in pagan mythology—not the tinkering of a god who hangs out most days on Mount Olympus but whips up a strategic thunderstorm for the Trojans now and then. This gets inside our space. It gets inside our lives.

When life is going great, most Christians don't let these metaphors get too close because we love our autonomy and feel as if we have a handle on things. But when chaos hits—when the nine-volt battery of our own ability finally fizzles out—we're at last ready to plug our electric cords into God's outlet. "Give me the juice!" we pray. "Live through me because I got nothin'."

Even in that moment of vulnerability, Paul's word choice may still look strange to us. "I delight in weaknesses,"[6] he wrote—but no, that's not the emotion we feel at all. At least not yet. In fact, "delight" is the very last thing we feel. We feel ashamed of ourselves, maybe. We feel desperate. We feel humiliated. But all of these emotions are just aftershocks of the downfall of our self-effort. They are tremors in the dust of an infrastructure that needed to collapse.

Instead, we are given passages like these to cast vision for a new and indwelt life:

It is no longer I who live, but Christ who lives in me. And the life I now live in the flesh I live by faith in the Son of God, who loved me and gave himself for me.[7]

I am the vine; you are the branches. Whoever abides in me and I in him, he it is that bears much fruit, for apart from me you can do nothing. If anyone does not abide in me he is thrown away like a branch and withers; and the branches are gathered, thrown into the fire, and burned. If you abide in me, and my words abide in you, ask whatever you wish, and it will be done for you.[8]

I have been crucified with Christ. It is no longer I who live, but Christ who lives in me.[9]

But we have this treasure in earthen vessels, that the excellency of the power may be of God, and not of us.[10]

If the weaknesses that you have found disgust and embarrass you, that's understandable. This happens to all of us at first, I think. But those emotions do not limit what God can do with your devastation. In fact, when you finally know that you aren't strong; when you finally know that you are lost; when you finally see that you can't heal your own life or anybody else's, you stand in the greatest spiritual potential you will ever have. In this admission, you can finally throw up your hands and grant permission for your Savior to do what the New Testament promises he will do over and over again—to move his life and will through us.

The Glory of the Weak

Glory is a word we don't use much these days, but it's an important biblical term that can connote weight, value, and brightness. In a world of digital currency, we rarely affiliate material mass and financial worth, but in biblical times, pounds of gold could determine the wealth of a king. This sort of glory is demonstrated in brilliance and heft. It's reflected in luminosity and in gravity.

In the third chapter of his second letter to the Corinthians, Paul described the difference between the glory of the laws of Moses and the glory of the work of Jesus. He said that the laws of the Old Testament were so weighty and so bright, the Israelites couldn't even look at Moses' face as he carried the commands of God. Yet as glorious as this law was, it faded over time. The law that condemns can only take us so far, so Paul wrote,

> For if there was glory in the ministry of condem-
> nation [the law], the ministry of righteousness [faith
> in Christ] must far exceed it in glory. Indeed, in this
> case, what once had glory has come to have no glory
> at all, because of the glory that surpasses it. For if
> what was being brought to an end came with glory,
> much more will what is permanent have glory.[11]

In other words, all the glory of our strained human effort to be good crumbles beside the glory that is freely given to us by Jesus. For traumatized people, this is particularly comforting. In times of chaos, we stand humiliated by our own failures because we've been hurt too deeply to perform for God. We watch all our good deeds slip like sand through our fingers and finally admit what we cannot accomplish for him. In this moment, Jesus offers us a stronger and better glory than anything we could have won on our own.

Paul wrote, "Therefore we do not lose heart, but though our outer man is decaying, yet our inner man is being renewed day by day. For momentary, light affliction is producing for us an eternal weight of glory far beyond all comparison."[12] What is this weight of glory? It's the substance (the lustrous bulk, the glimmering mass) of a gospel that secures what we can never secure in our own willpower. During the months and years of our affliction on earth, we cry out to the God who lives inside us, a God who knows what we aren't able to do, a God who stands ready to give us everything we need forever and ever.

I like how Sally Lloyd-Jones framed this picture of God in the opening of her *Jesus Storybook Bible*:

> Now, some people think the Bible is a book of rules, telling you what you should and shouldn't do. The Bible certainly does have some rules in it. They show you how life works best. But the Bible isn't mainly about you and what you should be doing. It's about God and what he has done. Other people think the Bible is a book of heroes, showing you people you should copy. The Bible does have some heroes in it, but (as you'll soon find out) most of the people in the Bible aren't heroes at all. They make some big mistakes (sometimes on purpose). They get

afraid and run away. At times they are downright
mean. No, the Bible isn't a book of rules, or a book
of heroes. The Bible is most of all a Story. It's an
adventure story about a young Hero who comes
from a far country to win back his lost treasure.
It's a love story about a brave Prince who leaves his
palace, his throne—everything—to rescue the one
he loves.[13]

Living out this rescue won't always be comfortable or easy.
In fact, Paul said,

> Meanwhile we groan, longing to be clothed instead
> with our heavenly dwelling, because when we are
> clothed, we will not be found naked. For while we
> are in this tent, we groan and are burdened, because
> we do not wish to be unclothed but to be clothed
> instead with our heavenly dwelling, so that what is
> mortal may be swallowed up by life.[14]

Simultaneously, Paul delighted in his temporal weakness
and groaned over the residue of his lingering mortality. He
knew that God's grace for him was sufficient, and he also
knew that this same grace had not finished all the work it
would eventually do inside him.

If you are living through chaos, don't feel alone. The
vertigo of this season is scary, and while you probably feel
vulnerable, you don't have to despair about the weaknesses

pain is revealing. As you walk through this valley of the shadow of death, the Lord is with you. You were saved, and you are still being saved. Even this end of your world will be used by the Father who loves you. You don't have to be God's little hero; in fact, it's okay if you collapse on your knees before the Almighty and say, "If I must boast, I will boast of the things that show my weakness." For here in this holy place where you are most weak, you are most strong.

Scared to Death: A Letter to the Fearful

"It's cancer."

My friend is normally chatty, but this morning her messages were broken as she struggled to tell me the details. For days, we had been waiting on her mom's test results, and here was the news we didn't want.

"I don't know what to do," she wrote.

"Want me to call you?" I asked.

"Not yet. I feel paralyzed. I can't even talk about it."

"I get that," I said. My mom had lung cancer last year, so I remember the shock of that first day.

"I'm stuck," she wrote.

"Of course you are," I said. "It's hard, hard news. It's hard to even get your brain around it."

"It doesn't even seem real!"

"I'm so sorry," I said.

The conversation went silent on the other end for a few minutes. I could tell she was reeling, so I just waited.

"Hey, will you let me give you a little bit of advice?" I finally asked.

"What?"

"I know that you want to sit in the same chair all day long and hold your breath until all this is over . . ."

"Yeah . . ."

"That's how shock works. You don't want to eat. Sleep is tough. Fear does crazy stuff to a body, so you're going to have to be intentional about taking care of yourself so you can take care of your mom. If I didn't live fifteen hours away, I'd bring you dinner, but I can send you a gift card and urge you to eat at least one decent meal today. And make yourself drink a bunch of water . . . do some deep stretches . . . take a walk outside. Get your blood moving so that your brain has oxygen to process whatever news you get."

"You're right," my friend wrote. "I can feel myself shutting down."

"I know, sweet girl. It's so scary. I'm so sorry."

If you've lived through a serious diagnosis, you know how hard it is to keep any sort of healthy routine. Nothing is simple when you are terrified. Your impulses get all twisted, and you can't rest easily. When you do sleep, you wake up at weird times. You lose your appetite. You wander through life in a daze, and weird things bother you.

When you go shopping, you wonder why anybody would argue with their kids over a box of fruit snacks. "Stop fighting over something so stupid!" you want to yell. "I'll buy them *for you*, but stop fighting! Don't you realize that people out there have cancer?" But you don't say that. You just choke back tears and try to remember what was next on your list.

For years, I've told hurting friends, "If you need me, I'm here," but now I know why scared people can't always talk it out. Talking through fear is nothing like talking through anger. It's more like falling off a swing—you're gasping and cramping, wondering if any of your rib bones are broken. You can't even move until your breath comes back to you.

When Mom was sick, so many friends asked me how I was doing, but as much as I appreciated their concern, I couldn't figure out how to answer that question. "How am I? My mom has cancer. That's how I am."

My mother is a point on my compass, a star that establishes my bearings in the night. She taught me how to create from scraps, how to chase the impossible, how to love persistently, how to fight fearlessly, and how to believe in Jesus like a child. She taught me how to milk this life for all it has to offer while holding my best efforts loosely because of the glory of the next world.

Her lung cancer was nowhere on my radar. She has never smoked, and she bikes twenty-one miles some days. She eats healthy. She's lived a clean life. On the night I got that terrible phone call, I stayed calm and said, "I love you," in my best fake brave voice, then I hung up the phone and started to google survival rates. As I scrolled through page after page on cancer.org, my heart felt as if it were trying to claw its way up and out of my throat.

The Complexity of Fear

As the strong emotions of fear wash over us, legitimate physiological reactions are also happening inside our bodies. While our mouths start to feel dry, as our hearts begin to pound, as our knees begin to quiver, we are experiencing changes in our endocrine, nervous, and immune systems. Most of these changes begin in the hypothalamic-pituitary-adrenal axis, a network comprised of "the hypothalamus, the anterior lobe of the pituitary gland, and the adrenal gland."[1] However, the "brain stem noradrenergic neurons, sympathetic adrenomedullary circuits, and parasympathetic systems" are also involved.[2] In other words, fear isn't just happening in some other-dimensional faith realm—it's happening inside the very real machines of our bodies.

Some of these biological responses are helpful in times of stress because they can make us more aware, help us think faster, and numb pain so that we are able to respond.[3] You've heard the term *fight or flight*, and that term captures the two responses most of us experience in times of danger. Other physiological responses prove detrimental, however, urging us to react poorly or freeze.

Once, I was chased through a wood by a man wielding a knife. As soon as I realized what was happening, the whole world seemed to slow down. I could think with utter clarity. I felt agile and ferocious. Within seconds, I had assessed my surroundings and developed strategies for both escape and counterattack.

Why was I able to do this? On a chemical level, adrenaline and norepinephrine were coursing through my veins almost instantly, then cortisol a few moments later. These hormones probably gave me the mental and physical boost I needed to get through the crisis.

Yet what if my body chemistry had reacted differently? Might I have frozen instead? Actually, yes. Rats from certain genetic lines exhibit *proactive* responses to a threat while others exhibit *reactive* responses, so it's at least possible that humans have an inborn, biological tendency to either run away or attack.[4] (You know that great-grandmother who told you that you were born with feisty Scottish blood? She might have been more accurate than you realized.)

How, then, do I interpret the scientific aspect of fear as a Christian? Often, when believers tell a dramatic story like mine, they claim that God intervened to help them survive. If they make it through a car wreck, God saved them. If they make it through a public shooting, God protected them. If they are able to think clearly in a moment of intense fear, God gave them insight. I understand why we make this assumption. My gratitude immediately rose to God when I realized I had escaped from that knife-wielding attacker. At the same time, I know that not everybody who loves Jesus—and not everybody who is *loved by* Jesus—escapes trauma. So if I claim that God did a miracle for me, am I also implying that he didn't perform a miracle for my dear friend who froze in her moment of need?

This is a delicate subject, but it's also an important one. As I have talked with other women over twenty years of ministry, I have regularly heard former abuse victims express self-hate for their own passivity. "Why didn't I fight harder? Why didn't I run faster? Why didn't I see that coming?" These questions haunt victims, a burden that may grow heavier if I flippantly claim that God gave me miraculous strength during my attack. What will a hurting friend believe about God's feelings toward her if I tell her that he gave *me* unique help during *my* time of need? And if I'm wrong—if God didn't perform a miracle for me—has my explanation been fair to her? If I were only a little more self-aware, a little more honest, a little more precise, could I save my friend some pain?

Still, being precise about God isn't always easy. How do we ever know for certain what God has or hasn't done? Prayer impacts the world, or God wouldn't have asked us to do it—but he doesn't usually give us a receipt proving the result of the exchange. "Feeling the Holy Spirit" might provide internal validation for us sometimes, but most older Christians can describe a time when they misinterpreted God because of their own emotions, proving that "spiritual tremors" are sometimes unreliable.

For a long time, I wrestled with all of these angles on fear and God's intervention. Then one day it hit me—dissecting the miraculous from the mundane isn't the primary goal of a believer. God is not sitting around waiting for me to give him credit for some divine activity that he's hidden inside obscurity. He's placed me inside a *miraculous whole*, a macro universe that operates according to his mind-blowing laws of biology, chemistry, and physics. Inside this miraculous whole, micro compressions of God's creative power—*miraculous instances*—sometimes display God's direct intervention. For example, on the same day that grapes grown by common grace were fermenting slowly in jugs (the miraculous whole), Jesus also turned one batch of water very quickly into wine (the miraculous instance).[5] *Both exist on the continuum of divine creation. Both testify to our Father's involvement in the universe.*

So if we *know for certain* that God has done something supernatural, we should talk about that story as a miracle. If we *think* God has done something supernatural, we should explain why we think so, without applying any sort of spiritual or emotional pressure to our listeners. If we just have a *hunch* that God intervened, we can tell our story in those terms. And if we really *don't know*, we can express the faith of a believer who walks inside a world that was created by God's very hand.

I'm making an argument for basic spiritual honesty here, a practice that would be easy and obvious if Christian culture hadn't developed bad habits of sensationalizing and embellishing testimony. If we've been exposed to exaggerated expectations very long, figuring out how to tell our stories honestly can take some work. But once we know that it's okay to stick with whatever we do and don't know, much of the confusion clears. If God's left something a mystery, we honor him when we talk about it as a mystery. If he has revealed a fact, we honor him when we talk about it as a fact. One of my favorite lines from an Andrew Peterson song says, "A thing resounds when it rings true."[6] In other words, people can tell if we are being deep-down real with them. The church doesn't need to be afraid of that sort of openness.

As we look at these biological and spiritual aspects of fear, another obvious truth begins to emerge. Exhorting others to be brave (as if fear were some sort of switch we could flip on and off at will) usually isn't helpful. You've probably seen the meme that says, "Never in the history of calming down has anyone ever calmed down by being told to calm down." That's funny (in a dark sort of way) because squashing fear isn't that simple for everyone.

In particular, smart and sensitive people with big imaginations can see zillions of possibilities for potential danger, which means they sometimes experience more worry. Several scientific studies suggest a possible connection between higher IQs and anxiety,[7] and students who score higher on verbal intelligence tests live with a greater sense of angst.[8] On the opposite side of the spectrum, the Darwin Award is an accolade given to individuals who remove themselves from the gene pool by doing something stupid. It's not a compassionate award to give, of course, but it operates on the general assumption that intelligent people usually see what's dangerous and avoid it. The upside of being a brain? Smarts might save your life. The downside? Geniuses might feel a little more fear now and then, causing constant stress that's bad for the body. This timidity can also lead to regret—a life commandeered by the trembling "What if?" is rarely lived to the full.

When the Bible speaks about fear—which is often—it speaks into all of this complexity. God knows your defaults. He knows your instincts. He knows your biology, your chemistry, your genetics, your experiences, and your intellectual capacity. Every connection that occurs in your nervous system, every fluid released by every gland, every physiological reaction—from the lump in your throat to the drop of your stomach—is seen by the God who made you.

This means that when Jesus comes to the believer saying, "Do not fear," he's not like humans who tell you not to worry. He understands what others cannot understand about us because he knows us back and forth, inside and out. He knows that for some of us, this is a command to walk on land, and for others, it's a command to walk on water.

The Silence of Love

My favorite apostle once wrote, "The Word became flesh and made his dwelling among us."[9] As a kid, I would skim over that verse, but one day it finally hit me—this is the guy who leaned against Jesus' breast during dinner. He must have valued human contact as I do.

During Christ's time on earth, John got close enough to hear his heartbeat. He felt God's warmth. He heard God's voice. He listened to him breathe. Seeing this intimacy makes me grieve for John. How hard it must have been for him to stand at the foot of the cross, watching his best friend's blood drip upon the dust—the same blood that he had heard thrumming through Christ's arteries and veins. This apostle said, "The Word became flesh," because he had leaned against that flesh, and he had seen it suffer and die.

Imagine watching the surprise on John's face when he finally put two and two together, realizing that the teacher he loved so dearly was actually a *God* who held the whole law of Moses inside a single human body. Thousands of years of festivals, prophecies, and sacrifices all complete in one divine person!

You've seen television shows in which a famous person hides in costume while mixing life up with regular folks. Then there's a big reveal with cheesy grins and shouts of laughter. "It's Adele!" That surprise would be nothing compared to John's shock when he suddenly realized he'd reclined upon the chest of the one who said, "Let there be light." He had sat next to the Messiah who trumped every wool-itchy law. The metaphors and the shadows, the incense and the smoke, the curtains of the Temple had all converged in a single living being who walked on the earth as close as a mother.

Once you get beyond Christ's suffering and death to the Resurrection, the phrase "the Word became flesh" feels almost like a punch line. (Pa-dum-dum!) Surely John smiled while writing down those words, remembering three close years that had come and gone, and then feeling a deep homesickness in his chest. There he had stood, feet on the earth, looking up into the sky and watching his best friend rise out of touch and out of sight. The Holy Spirit's arrival was beautiful, of course; Pentecost was glorious in a whole different way. Still, if I had been John, I would have wanted both the Comforter and the Creator—the inner light and the outer light, the seen and the unseen.

I definitely wanted as much of God as I could get during Mom's cancer. And you know, some days, God did feel tactile. During those times, God's Spirit provided tangible reassurance that is difficult to describe. His comfort was vivid and sweet, and after basking in that soul warmth, I could understand how eternity with Jesus would offer utter contentment.

This strong awareness of God's presence wasn't constant, though, which was painful. On days when I searched for emotional confirmation of his closeness and found little peace or comfort, silence felt like a betrayal—as if he'd let me down when I most needed him. I knew he had given me the Bible and that I should look for him there, but I wanted something more, well, human. More than once I prayed, "Why won't you talk to me audibly? Is that against some sort of rule? Why would you withhold something so easy from me when I need it so badly? I need the sound of you."

When I was a little girl, I heard older Christians talk about feeling God's closeness, and for a long time, I assumed that those people who raved about their mystical experiences were more mature in the faith. Now I'm not so sure. In fact, in chapter 8 of *The Screwtape Letters*, C. S. Lewis makes the opposite argument—saying that God allows certain Christians to walk through troughs that contain no sign of his existence because he has a special plan for their growth. In Lewis's fictional story, a senior demon (Screwtape) is advising his nephew (Wormwood) how to tempt human beings. The following scene explains Lewis's theory on God's silence. (Keep in mind that demons are talking, which makes their "Enemy," of course, God.) Uncle Screwtape writes,

> *You [Wormwood] must have often wondered why the Enemy [God] does not make more use of His power to be sensibly present to human souls in any degree He chooses and at any moment.* But you now see that the Irresistible and the Indisputable are the two weapons which the very nature of His scheme forbids Him to use. Merely to override a human will (as His felt presence in any but the faintest and most mitigated degree would certainly do) would be for Him useless. He cannot ravish. He can only woo. For His ignoble idea is to eat the cake and have it; the creatures are to be one with Him, but yet themselves; merely to cancel them, or assimilate them, will not serve. He is prepared to do a little overriding at the beginning. He will set them off with communications of His presence which,

though faint, seem great to them, with emotional sweetness, and easy conquest over temptation. But He never allows this state of affairs to last long. Sooner or later He withdraws, if not in fact, at least from their conscious experience, all those supports and incentives. He leaves the creature to stand up on its own legs—to carry out from the will alone duties which have lost all relish. *It is during such trough periods, much more than during the peak periods, that it is growing into the sort of creature He wants it to be. Hence the prayers offered in the state of dryness are those which please Him best.* We can drag our patients along by continual tempting, because we design them only for the table, and the more their will is interfered with the better. He cannot 'tempt' to virtue as we do to vice. *He wants them to learn to walk and must therefore take away His hand; and if only the will to walk is really there He is pleased even with their stumbles.* Do not be deceived, Wormwood. *Our cause is never more in danger than when a human, no longer desiring, but still intending, to do our Enemy's will, looks round upon a universe from which every trace of Him seems to have vanished, and asks why he has been forsaken, and still obeys.*[10]

As I sat beside my mother post-op, watching every breath and checking her pulse oximeter, I wished that the tactile presence of Jesus would never ebb or fade. I wished that the Holy Spirit would hook me up, Matrix-style, to a constant saline flow of "There you are" instead of teaching me maturity in my faith during a hard time. But as fear grabbed me around the throat, I slowly learned to make non-emotive decisions about the trustworthiness of my King. Even as cortisol and adrenaline pulsed through my veins, even as my heart rate increased, even as my breathing grew shallow, I learned that no matter what the machine of my body feels, I'm always indwelt by the Holy Spirit, and that I always have access to all of God's resources—resources that are activated by trust instead of by emotion.

And when I trembled and silently asked God if he was there, when I expressed frustration that he was quiet, I found that he still loved me. His grace was big enough to sustain me while I wobbled in my belief. Of course, my underdeveloped faith muscles got sore because I wasn't used to activating certain parts of my spirit so much or so intensely. But, like a father teaching his daughter to ride a bike, God supported me some, let me fall some, helped me get back up. He went through that process with me in real time so that I would learn to ride faster and stronger in freedom.

I never once liked it when traces of God seemed to vanish, but on the other side of Mom's cancer, I can see how necessary those moments were to my growth. Confusing stretches in which God seemed to withdraw strengthened my faith in ways that constant spiritual highs could never have accomplished.

They Say They Had a Peace about It

For years, I have heard religious people say, "I had a peace about it," while trying to prove that a decision or belief was affirmed by God. I think I get what they're trying to say. Sometimes I have felt a deep sense of calm while following Jesus. But as nice as this sensation is, I'm not convinced that this emotion proves a reliable indicator of God's will.

Maybe after decades of walking in the Spirit, as our union with God increases, our emotions will begin to align more naturally with the truth of God. But even if this happens, I don't think humans ever get to the point in which a feeling of peacefulness can be trusted more than the Word of God. In fact, I know of specific claims of "peacefulness" that could not have resulted from God's blessing.

When a powerful man argued that God had given him peace about having sex with a vulnerable young woman, he was wrong. God didn't give him that peace. That may have been an endorphin rush—but it wasn't the Holy Spirit. Another time I heard a pastor say that he "had peace about" dishonest and divisive behavior that wrecked a church. He sounded so confident when he described his sense of calling, never admitting that God wouldn't lead one of his followers to operate in deceit. Likewise, I have seen the phrase "God spoke to me" misapplied so many times, often by people who want something so badly, they are willing to project their own desire onto the Lord. Feeling positive about something doesn't equal a divine calling, and we are wise to be wary when this assumption appears.

I know this struggle from the inside, too, because my own heart has been just as hypocritical at times. During a lonely and excruciating time of my life, I blamed the Lord for rules that were "too hard to keep." I waded into the shallow waters of sins that relieved some of my suffering temporarily, and the relief that flooded my heart was so shockingly powerful that I let myself imagine that God wouldn't care if I dived the whole way in—or even that he might have a special plan for me that involved an unconventional choice. Looking back on that, I realize that what I called "peacefulness" was actually just the pleasure of running away from difficulty. A marathon runner who gives up at mile nineteen might feel a rush of sudden relief. Standing up to take a few more steps might be agony. But the delight that comes in quitting isn't equivalent to the full peace of finishing the race.

If we go back to the Scriptures, we can find lots of people who had what we call "peacefulness" in times of disobedience. The prophet Jonah slept soundly on a boat while running away from the command of God. The people of Sodom cast aside self-reflection to live in indulgence on the eve of their destruction. The disciples slept in the garden after Jesus asked them to stay awake with him. Jeremiah 6 describes a rebellious nation that had forgotten to blush, people who could not even feel shame about their sins but who cried out "Peace, peace" when there was no peace.[11]

Jesus, on the other hand, wasn't always tranquil. In the garden, he cried out, and he sweated blood, and he wept. David wasn't peaceful while writing many of the Psalms.

Jeremiah wasn't calm during his laments. Timothy felt nervous when he was called to be strong. Paul struggled with depression, even when he was leading the church on the best possible path. When we examine all this together, we must admit that whatever the "peace of God" that guards our hearts and our minds in Christ Jesus[12] is, it's not an instant shot of the warm fuzzies. Sometimes doing wrong can feel right. Sometimes following God's leadership can feel strained and foreign to us.

So when feelings of fear, anxiety, or restlessness do hit, it's important to see them for what they are. They aren't indications that God has abandoned us. They aren't indications that we have messed up or that we are on the wrong track. They are emotions to address. That's all.

The Danger of Comparison

In the midst of fear, we also need to be careful about comparing our emotions with the emotions of others. In groups of nonreligious people, you will find some who are *naturally bold*. Certain personalities are just born risk-takers, not prone to thinking through consequences. Then there are *rationalists* who rarely allow themselves to be driven by feelings of any sort. Strategy is their default, not their instinct, so panic doesn't hit them in the same way as it might hit a feeler. *Feelers*, on the other hand, may find themselves moved quickly and easily by circumstances or emotions. Tranquility isn't on the emotional playlist as often as excitement, giddiness, sorrow, and fury.

Some of these inborn personality differences are impacted by personal choice, but chemical and genetic factors also come into play. God makes some people with a high natural capacity for analysis, others with a high natural capacity for risk, others with a high natural capacity for sensitivity. Instead of feeling pride or shame over our wiring, we can just acknowledge our defaults, seeing them as tools in a toolbox. We can acknowledge the pros and cons of our personalities and then ask God how he wants us to move forward.

So if you struggle with fear while someone in your religious community brags about his or her boldness, don't let that comparison go too deep. This difference might not result from spiritual maturity so much as chemical capacity. And besides that, you serve a God who isn't limited by your fear. In fact, it's possible that your inborn sensitivity is vital to the specific work God has prepared for you.

Marching Orders

So what do we do with all those "Do not fear" commands? Did the God who made our adrenal systems and personalities really think we could avoid *feeling* scared?

Maybe you aren't like this, but so often when I hear a command, I try to jump right into spiritual performance. I try to *be* a Christian as I try to diet, declaring, "I need to get a grip on this!" But honestly, changing myself spiritually usually goes about as well as trying not to eat an open pack of

Oreos in my pantry. So what if instead of shaming ourselves for our feelings, trying to pull ourselves up by our bootstraps and hating ourselves when we fail, we took time to admit the real truth of our situation to God? What if we just said, "Lord, I am scared. I need some help with this fear"? This is a powerful step to take because the gospel isn't about working harder to prove ourselves—it's about the power of God living through incapable humans.

Too often humans use the Bible's "Do not fear" verses to beat up trembling Christians, but what if God gave those words to us as reassurances of existing truth instead of cold commands that we are left alone to follow? Maybe he isn't trying to shame us but comfort us. In fact, if you trace most of those commands back or forward a bit, you'll find immediate connections to God's presence, affection, and love. For example: "Do not fear, *for I am with you.*"[13] "*Perfect love* casts out fear."[14] "Don't be afraid; *you are worth more than many sparrows.*"[15]

In a few instances—like the account of the storm on the sea—Christ seems to be putting a hard finger in the ribs of the trembling, but a great many biblical commands regarding fear don't work like statements of rebuke so much as reminders that God sees and cares deeply for us. They are words to reorient instead of words to rebuke.

When I was scared at night as a little girl, one of my parents would come to my room and say, "Don't worry. I'm here. It's okay." Mom and Dad didn't berate me. They didn't stand at the foot of my bed and yell, "What's wrong with you, kid? What kind of parent do you think I am that I wouldn't keep you safe? I'm so disgusted with you for being scared. Get over it, will you?" Of course not. They knew I was just a little kid who had a lot to learn. They counteracted my fear with a reassurance that they were near. They reminded me over and over again, "We're here. We love you." I never got tired of hearing this reaffirmation from my parents as a little girl, and as an adult, I never get tired of reminders about the closeness of my God.

Corrie ten Boom is one of my favorite writers because her words allow me to be very honest about my feelings while also redirecting my focus to a personal and paternal heavenly Father. She once wrote, "Never be afraid to trust an unknown future to a known God,"[16] and I love this statement because it resonates with the truth of Psalm 119:114: "You are my hiding place and my shield; I hope in your word." *You* are my hiding place. The answer to fear is found in a person.

I need to hear this reminder over and over again because I gravitate to hyperanalytical theology that distracts me from the childlike trust of burying myself in Jesus. But mastering fear isn't an intellectual technique. It's not a proverb or a spiritual equation. It's accepting all of our limitations of chemistry, personality, and environment while moving deeper and deeper into God. This God has let me come to the ends of my human courage and religious determination so many times, and as I stare over that precipice, I always see how much I need him. I don't just need him theoretically, I need him practically. Real time. Real person. There at the end of myself, I pray, "I'm scared, God! Where are you?" which turns into "Oh! You're here." Then at last, I sigh, "You are enough!" But every time, this seems to be a discovery instead of a profession.

Two Worlds, One Lesson

During Mom's cancer, God loved me enough to keep me in parallel worlds: the world of a hospital with scientific risks, medical procedures, and animal adrenaline—and the world of the Kingdom of Heaven, with its long, straight vision into eternity. He gave me his silent, tactile presence some moments. Other moments, he let me feel as if I were falling.

There were a few days when I felt as if I could face anything because I could see the Kingdom of God so clearly. Other days my knees shook so badly, I could hardly walk another lap on the second floor of a Florida hospital. This combination gave me just enough courage to take one reluctant, terrified step after another, strengthening muscles that grew with every movement.

As far as I can tell, twelve baskets of fish and bread weren't left over from that experience. I didn't emerge as a spiritual superstar with a story fit for *The 700 Club*; however, feeling fear while learning faith showed me that no matter what I felt, and no matter how intensely I felt it, God's arms were always wrapped around me. He allowed me to stretch in uncomfortable ways that helped me grow, and his love has made room for me in every state—whether I was a blubbering disciple who couldn't get enough of him or a bleary-eyed, worn-out pilgrim who desperately needed to be reminded that he was there.

Even the silence of God came around to feel like love in the end. It didn't feel like love in the middle, and it certainly didn't in the beginning, but in retrospect, his fingerprints were all over my growing pains, and his voice was in those wordless whispers that arose out of the quiet. In all of this, I was never alone. In all of this, I was loved.

Christ is strong enough for your fear too, so if you feel weak right now, I hope you won't be ashamed of your weakness. Life can be scary, especially if you love big, and it can be difficult to see how frightening times will ever be purposeful. The dialogue surrounding fear in some religious communities makes these seasons even more difficult, heaping guilt and shame upon our weary hearts. So if you read this letter trembling, I hope you will know that "Do not fear" isn't a hoop for you to jump through; it's a reminder that God hasn't abandoned you. It's a whisper from a loving parent who may sometimes use silence to grow us, but who is always as close as our own breath.

The Kiss of the Mountain God: A Letter to the Skeptical

I was one of those over-thinky kids who looked for metaphors everywhere. Whenever I was outside, I expected to read nature like a theology book. A soft rain meant God was close. A covering of thick moss showed me that he was gentle. The sharp smell of pine needles reminded me that divinity was unbridled. I thought I could find God's guidance anywhere if I could just listen well enough to what his creation had to say. After all, the book of Romans tells us that God's attributes of eternal power and divine nature are revealed through the created order.

Yet, one afternoon when I was about six or seven, I was sitting at the kitchen table when one of those mammoth houseflies landed right next to my hand and died. Boom. The impact didn't kill the thing; he just ran out of life at that precise moment. One second he was buzzing around, and the next he was belly up with all six legs in the air. Bzzzzzrt. Dead. The whole scene could have been part of a dark British comedy.

That experience wouldn't create a spiritual crisis for a lot of people, but it threw little-kid me for a loop. Until that moment, the world had seemed pregnant with the goodness of God, and here was a dead fly knocking me off my game. The ugliness and pointlessness of his demise didn't align with the holy romance I had always found in planet Earth.

"What does this *mean*?" I prayed. "Is the world really so random?"

I was just a kid, so I hadn't read any existentialists at that age, of course—but here was the epistemological seed of *Waiting for Godot* or "The Metamorphosis." This dead fly felt like a flash of hard, adult reality, a look behind the Matrix or behind the Wizard's curtain in Oz. Even at that early age, it pushed me to ask if the universe had any significance at all.

Yeah, these were weird, childish thoughts, but they were also part of the fundamental decision we all have to make when trying to reconcile what makes sense about the world with what feels meaningless. I regularly see friends post photos of a sunrise with the hashtag #Godisgood, and I get what they mean. But last Sunday a baby fawn was hit by a car at the end of our driveway, and today he was mostly eaten by buzzards. His tiny mouth was jacked open so that flies could buzz in and out of it. What hashtag should I use for that? It's the same natural world, but sometimes it's ugly instead of beautiful.

A couple of years ago, the Internet was riddled with pictures of "Get Well Soon!" balloons tied to the legs of dead animals on the side of the road. College kids with a dark sense of humor would find a rigor mortis ground-hog or a sun-drying possum and attach these Mylar well-wishes for all to see. Get well soon? Impossible. It's too late, and the hopelessness of the situation is the punch line of the joke. There's no getting better this time. Dark humor, yes, but it's also a nod to a tension I feel constantly. Can my faith really make poetry out of road pizza? Should it even try? How does God fit into a world that's so ugly sometimes?

Because there are days when the grim realities of earth turn far more serious than a dead groundhog. We live in an era of mass shootings, embolisms in young mothers, and accidents that didn't have to happen. God allows all this. He doesn't stop it. And when my heart rips in half in empathy, I think, *Why? What could possibly be the eternal significance of such a terrible thing?*

One day I can be overwhelmed with the glory of the earth and the next day stunned by the horror of it. While I'm listening to Rich Mullins sing about the fury of the pheasant's wings showing us how the Lord is in his temple,[1] I may fall to my knees. In such moments, nature reads like a prophecy that points straight into the Holy of Holies. Forty-eight hours later, though, I can watch a NOVA special and see a band of wild dogs attacking a wounded animal, and creation feels cold, void, material, and indifferent.

Wendell Berry once claimed that the Lord "goes fishing every day / in the Kentucky River. I see Him often,"[2] and these lines make me smile because I, too, have met with my Lord where waves smack against the sides of a metal fishing boat. But I have had dead times too—times when I felt like a naked ape wearing 50+ sunscreen, not sensing transcendence at all. What do I do with these wild extremes? When do I apply Romans 1 to the created order, looking for evidence of God's nature? And when do I let a dead fly be a dead fly?

This choice seems to be easy for two types of people. Depending on theological bias, either they filter out ugliness and embrace beauty as a sign of God's love, or they ignore the wonders of the earth and announce that God is dead. But a third type also exists—people who are weary from a tension we rarely talk about. Whether we are atheists or Christians, reason has driven us to conclusions about how the universe works, and we argue those conclusions with passion. Yet underneath that surface, the affective side of our nature won't let go of a secret, internal conflict. If God is love, does my theological argument for the existence of evil really justify all that happens around me? And if God is dead, why is the universe so pregnant with glory?

The Many Languages of God

I woke up around four to sit with my dad in his jon boat on Lake Barkley. The whole world was dark except for a new moon whose reflection lay on the surface of the water like a child's glass of milk. Still waters feel fragile, so I held my breath, afraid that any movement might splosh light over the cup edges into the clean, black deep.

A water strider cut straight through the moon's reflection, dividing it into rungs of a staircase that looked as if it might lead to heaven. I didn't see angels ascend and descend those steps, but a barred owl flapped strong wings twice slowly over the water while the heron and the egret coughed and jabbered through their morning prayers. A snapping turtle's nose rose, and she stared at me with cold, black eyes before sinking back down below. When a carp jumped, she left a beaded curtain of the river behind her. She frolicked like David in his ephod, dancing before the Lord with all his might.[3]

Dad used the trolling motor to turn a bend, and in a crook of a wooded island, we found dozens of slender columns of steam rising like a choir of fog angels. The ancient Greeks wrote stories about naiads, river nymphs who were bound to the waters. But this morning, I saw the river rinsing her long, pretty arms in a morning bath. How eagerly she yielded to the sun. I was almost jealous of her trust. Clouds ran the length of the sky, and as the morning kicked its feet through their cover, the day was born. My spirit shifted and rolled like a belly full of life, and something inside me felt Emmanuel, the Light of the World, was with us. He was, and he is, and he will return.

What I just described happened to me a couple of years ago, but I'm not sure how it will impact you to read it. It could move you. It could bore you. It could even infuriate you. During drought seasons of my walk with God, reading poetic descriptions of other people's "Jesus moments" made me feel frustrated and lonely. When the heavens seemed dry and empty, I was irritated by Christian "gushers" drunk on their own imaginations.

When I asked these gushers how they knew they were engaging with the Lord, they would say something like "Well, I can't explain it. I just *sense* God."

Those words did nothing but make me feel suspicious and alone.

When we are living in a time of spiritual famine, it can be painful to sit in the presence of those who talk about their own feast. Perhaps J. I. Packer was being sensitive to this when he said that describing his prayer life would be like telling someone how he made love to his wife.[4] His rebuke has made me think about how writers talk about their personal engagements with the Almighty. What stories should be kept private? What stories should be told? I'm still not sure.

Describing our faith is complicated in part because of a cultural shift that's happened inside Protestantism in recent years. In the '90s and early 2000s, a flurry of Christian training programs, seminars, and books promised to equip believers intellectually so that they could engage with an increasingly secular world. Rational arguments and strategies for spiritual multiplication were sometimes valued more than active dependence upon prayer. Logic wasn't just used as a tool of the faith; in some circles, it held the same importance as faith. Young believers were given evidence, rebuttals, and warnings as primary training for engagement with non-Christians. Not only did secular evolutionists debate Christian creationists, but internal conflict also arose between theistic evolutionists and young-earth Christians. Calvinists debated Arminians. Covenant theologians debated dispensationalists. Angry discernment bloggers reveled in lambasting every instance of theological error.

As all of this was under way, the political wing of American Christianity became more and more powerful. Pastors strategized with politicians. Masses of believers were corralled to work as advocates for or against legislation, and the public perception of Christianity shifted from a means of offering intimate connection to a living God to a pragmatic sociopolitical force.

I believe most of these efforts were rooted in sincere attempts to implement the faith in culture, but many believers felt thrashed about in these waves of reform, especially when the church valued winning cultural power more than winning souls. Then, as it always does, the pendulum began to swing in the opposite direction.

Gen Xers and Millennials value experience, so new generations of adult believers arose, ready to set the heavy polemics aside and find an irenic approach to sharing Jesus with the world. They valued honesty, conversation, beauty, mystery, service, and transcendence—traditional spiritual principles that were being squeezed out of a hyperpoliticized church. Yet in their zeal, a new hierarchy of spirituality was inadvertently created. The Internet allowed articulate but untrained believers to amass scads of fans, and in some venues, emotional and expressive writing began to trump theological accuracy. The warm-fuzzy "Jesus experience" felt close and real, though some of the principles undergirding these teachings were unorthodox.

Whereas some in the previous generation had squelched the gospel by elevating the human *mind*, some in the present generation reduced the gospel by elevating human *emotion*. As the poet was exalted over the God who sometimes uses poetry, many holy complexities of the I AM were lost.

The church has been swinging back and forth between theological and political extremes for centuries, so this sort of correction/overcorrection cycle is nothing new. Yet, as my favorite college professor said over and over again, "It's vital to know where you are in history." If we could perhaps look around and see why our impulses work the way they do, if we could just see why we feel a certain itch, we might be able to recognize the extremes that tempt us before they distort our message. And if we will center our trust deeply and actively in Jesus, he can guide us around those urges to play god that continually woo our hearts.

With this Christ-centered focus, the world can encounter

a church that isn't just a politicized machine or a bohemian soiree but a divinely indwelt body comprised of many different gifts and personalities. In this church, the world will find a God who moves the human heart, soul, mind, and strength, a God who reflects a little differently—though coherently—through each of his children. This diversity will hold to essential orthodoxy, of course, but its expressions may be as ergonomic as Mark's Gospel when expressed through an engineer, as metaphorical as John in a literature teacher, as tender as Luke in a physician, or as historical as Matthew in a lawyer.

Because of this ideal of Christ-centered complexity, it's unlikely that a single chapter of a single writer's book will connect with all skeptics. One human voice can't speak to the whole world, nor should it. If you and I are wired differently, if we see the world through disparate lenses, or even if we are walking through unique struggles, my story might not do anything for you. If you fail to connect with my viewpoint, that doesn't mean something is wrong with you. Even if several of your friends read this book and recommend it to you, God hasn't abandoned you if my story leaves you dry. God is a big God who speaks many languages, and he is likely to use someone besides me to tend you somewhere down the road, so I'm praying for that moment in your life, knowing that however it comes, his work is a beautiful thing.

Also, I want to limit the scope of what I'm going to attempt in this chapter. For the sake of space, I've decided to leave out most of the historical/textual research that accompanied my journey through skepticism. There's just not room here to get into all those nerdy diversions into Horus, Mithras, and Osiris; wrestling matches with Eastern logic and philosophy; and genre studies of Hebrew literature. In making that cut, I don't want to imply that my journey was limited to what I'm including here. If you are a literary/historical person who is now stuck in the middle of that sort of digging, please don't feel alone. This journey makes for a daunting endeavor, but I found Jesus at the end of it. Maybe someday I'll get the chance to tell you that part of the story as well.

The Renovation of a Skeptic
The End of Belief in Self

In the second chapter of *Orthodoxy*, G. K. Chesterton wrote, "Shall I tell you where the men are who believe most in themselves? . . . I can guide you to the thrones of the Super-men. The men who really believe in themselves are all in lunatic asylums. . . . A man will certainly fail, because he believes in himself. Complete self-confidence is not merely a sin; complete self-confidence is a weakness."[5]

Chesterton's words stand in fierce opposition to most teachings of the modern world. Almost every day we are told to believe in ourselves, to follow our hearts, to trust our gut, to do what feels good. Most of the movies we watch, most of the commercials we see, most of the self-help advice that we are given relies upon this ethic. What's the underlying drive here? While physical pleasure might seem like the big allure, there's in fact a pull stronger than hedonism at play. The more intoxicating promise is *safety*—safety that we can guarantee without having to trust anybody else.

I get the appeal of this promise. At several points in my life, I have been so disappointed with the church, with my relationships, and even with my faith, that I have wanted to hide inside myself forever. Yet, this has never worked because an insular body of water grows stagnant. Disappointment becomes bitterness; bitterness becomes cynicism; and cynicism is the booby prize of a fallen world—a sad, small bounty.

Examine the "believe in yourself" doctrine closely, and you will find Eve longing for a forbidden piece of fruit—not because one pear can ever be as lush as an entire garden, but because one pear is tiny enough to clutch in the palm of one small hand. This single pear represents all self-trust, an eternal folding inward, an eternal reduction.

What does a rejection of self-belief look like? Well, it certainly doesn't mean that we must embrace the "I am a worm" mentality that pervades too many pockets of Christianity. Our identity is changed when we receive Christ, and once we are a new creation, indwelt by the Spirit, it's not healthy to buy into ugly lies that hold us back. A Christian's confidence doesn't reside in "I'm great" but in "Greatness lives in me." *We don't withdraw trust but transfer it to what is trustworthy.* Theological grounding in our new nature helps skepticism die because it rescues us from the double dangers of stagnant self-confidence and paralyzing insecurity. I don't have this concept mastered yet, but I've lived with it long enough to realize how much can change when we think properly about ourselves.

The Way I Wanted It

While the main message of the Bible is so simple a child can catch it, certain sections of Scripture can be incredibly difficult to interpret. Historical, linguistic, and cultural research is needed before we can even begin to understand what certain pieces of the Word actually mean—and even if we do all this, sometimes our eyes just won't open to a truth until God is ready for us to see it.

When I was younger, I didn't like this at all. I've always been a quick, strong reader, so I expected the Bible to fall into place easily. I'd never met a book I couldn't master almost instantly, so I was frustrated that God (of all beings) would give me a snarly and complicated text instead of making his words entirely straightforward. I was also impatient, unwilling to let the *clear* teachings of the Bible assure me that the *unclear* would someday make sense as well.

Several decades later, most of my major questions about the text have cleared away. But in those early years, I expected an ethical God to work only on my terms. I was smart, proud, and certain, and I felt comfortable making demands. It took years for me to admit that an omnipotent God might have good reason for veiling some truths while revealing others. And it took years for me to realize that a living and active text would sometimes hold its secrets back, only to reveal them intentionally at a more meaningful season of my life. By this, my relationship with the Bible has changed. I bulldoze it less. I let it lead me more.

In this more trusting approach to the Word, I've begun to realize the artistic genius of the Scripture as a whole. Because I teach literature, I spend most of my year digging around in archaic texts. Nothing I have ever studied or taught works like the Bible. Between thirty-five and forty different authors wrote the books of the Bible over a span of about 1,500 years. The genres offered in its pages range from poetry, to history books, to legal books, to prophecies, to narratives, to letters. It's difficult for a single author working in one genre to create narrative unity, so it's truly astonishing that such a complicated text could adhere well enough to tell a single story. As someone who is trained to look for disparate elements of literature, I know that the Bible could never exist if it were not divinely inspired. Knowing that doesn't clear up all my questions, but it does provide a rock-solid foundation upon which to ask them.

Once I heard a *Star Wars* fan complaining about a Han Solo line suggesting that the *Millennium Falcon* made a trip in twelve parsecs. "A parsec measures distance, not time," he said. It's a legitimate complaint. But then again, these are movies with a Chewbacca in them. You don't walk into a new *Star Wars* film demanding fossil evidence for Ewoks; you go in willing to embrace the narrative as a whole. Sure, I might notice an errant term here and there, but I don't storm out of the theater because of it. I let the gap fall into a bigger context of a good story.

I've not always been willing to give the Bible this sort of trust. I don't mean to imply that the Bible contains errors, but even in its coherence, it contains difficult paradoxes that are impossible for a casual reader to untangle. I still get stumped in Deuteronomy and Leviticus sometimes, and I cannot understand why God did some of the things he did in the Old Testament. While the core of the Bible is so simple a child may catch it, certain elements of Scripture can present complex challenges to thoughtful and detailed readers. When we meet those challenges, we can proudly grab a couple of verses out of context and rage that "the God of the Bible is unethical and backward," but that's poor scholarship; a sloppy and lazy approach that ignores the great force of credibility established by the rest of the text. So I've grown to trust him despite what I cannot interpret yet. I'm learning that it's the sort of book you can understand in broad strokes at a first read, then go on to investigate deeply for decades. By it, you can meet the Good Shepherd at ten, the Psalms at twenty, Isaiah at thirty, Revelation at fifty, all the while nourished on the God who lives and grows inside us.

The Wisdom of Fools

During the pinnacle of my skepticism, I also failed to realize that every *natural* operation of the physical world is *supernatural* in a sense, for all that *is* was made from nothing. Every moment of our lives, we are baptized in the habitual grandeur of wonders that have grown invisible to us. As Robert Capon wrote, "Only miracle is plain; it is the ordinary that groans with the unutterable weight of glory."[6]

When the heavens proclaim the majesty of God, when our baby star seems to rise over the cusp of our infant planet every morning, the revelation means nothing to us. We yawn and hit snooze, trying to ignore it. Only when God breaks this grand rhythm once in all of human history for Joshua's army do we take any sort of notice.

Uneducated men embrace Joshua's impossible story by faith, and we call them fools because they don't understand interplanetary rotation or gravitational pull. But in their simplicity, they see what we fail to notice—that any force mighty enough to establish natural laws would also be sovereign over them.

We also fail to realize that if 2,400 years of Western philosophy have taught us anything, it's that human knowledge isn't watertight. What the rationalists failed to validate by logic, the empiricists failed to validate by experience. When the nihilists showed up to prove that nothing could be proven (a self-contradictory premise), we were left with the existentialists to comfort us. The best they could do? Tell us that we are free to create our own meaning. I think this is why suicide often follows existentialism so closely—we grow weary under a weight human shoulders were never meant to carry.

Christ stands ready to help us with this burden. He will let us try to carry it, of course; he will let us try to pick ourselves up off the earth by our own bootstraps, but when we are exhausted from this effort, he can lift the damnable humanistic weight that requires us to answer every single riddle. He will invite us to explore the world sincerely, granting us a reality in which the infinite is allowed to be infinite.

The older I get, the more I appreciate the very practical nature of Christ's claim: "I am the Truth"—a bold assertion that all truth emanates from a living being. After chasing so many other methodologies, I see that it's possible to find pieces of truth in one discipline or another, but apart from Christ, those pieces never seem to align properly into a coherent whole. Without orientation in the Truth Incarnate, we are five blind men trying to describe an elephant. Perhaps this is what C. S. Lewis meant when he said, "I believe in Christianity as I believe that the Sun has risen, not only because I see it, but because by it I see everything else."[7]

Two Things I Missed

WHAT WOULD THE WORLD LOOK LIKE IF THE BIBLE WERE TRUE?
Twenty years ago, most of the people I talked with agreed that human beings had a sinful nature. In fact, one of the most common Christian pamphlets ever printed taught that "man is sinful and separated from God" as the entry point to explaining the gospel.

Two decades ago, it was rare to find anyone—believer or non—who kicked back on that point. The zeitgeist agreed that something was inherently wrong with people in general. However, over the past twenty years, that assumption has become increasingly rare. Humans now feel more bold about their natural urges and desires. If someone calls our impulses evil, we are much more likely to cross our arms over our chests and demand, "Who says I'm wrong?" than to hang our heads and say, "You're right. Something is broken inside me."

If you're familiar with Brené Brown's TED Talk on shame,[8] you already know how she separates shame and guilt. According to Brown, "shame" says that *we* are bad while "guilt" says that *we have done a bad thing*. Right or wrong, this difference will automatically appeal to the postmodern thinker because we hate the idea of being inherently flawed. We can admit making a mistake, but we refuse to admit that we have made a mistake of ourselves.

What does the Bible say about all this? The orthodox view of sin claims human nature was damaged long ago with a single mistake made by Adam and Eve, a mistake that infected all of their offspring. That sounds bizarre until we examine what the error actually was. Satan told Eve that she could become godlike without staying in a dependent, obedient relationship with God, and she liked the idea of being her own sovereign. So she chose to trust her own wisdom more than she chose to trust her Maker's.

If this actually happened thousands of years ago, if that single tendency got passed down from a first generation to every person alive, what would humanity look like today? Well, at our core, we should all have a fundamental itch to be godlike without God. If Eve actually did what the Bible says she did, modern humans should crave autonomy and hate authority; we should revel in our own strength and despise our weaknesses (or excuse them); we should boast about planting our two feet proudly on a tiny square of grass, despite the fact that this little plot of earth is stuck to a warm rock flung 'round a tiny fireball on a thin string of space-time, a string measured in just enough miles to keep our guts from boiling.

If the Fall actually happened, modern critics of Christianity would still be using the "Hath God really said?" temptation as their primary springboard. They would continually flatter humans, keeping them drunk on promises of their own independence and glory while sowing cynicism about any teaching that asks for humility or submission.

The posture of Eden's serpent was "Oh, you silly thing. Do you really believe all that nonsense?" So if the Fall is true, this same whisper should now infiltrate every created discipline. It should worm its way into biology, chemistry, ethics, and physics. The "Hath God really said?" should slither and hiss its way past every indication of divine creation left in the natural order. It should ignore the unlikeliness of a clotting cascade springing up whole from nothing, ignore the implausibility of those first strands of RNA standing up to march, ignore the fact that the passage of billions of years cannot protect materialist theories from needing just as much magic as any mythical tale told around primitive fires. The hypnotic voice of the serpent should woo humans into a trance, singing sweetly about huge passages of time and remote possibilities, corralling all consciousness away from the fact that a life destined to die feels as if it were made to live.

If the Fall is true, today's psychological alchemists should tell me over and again that my flesh is god-flesh, that my will is god-will, that my desire is god-desire, that I am the master of my own destiny. They should insist upon this, even if I live in a culture full of people who can't seem to lose twenty extra pounds, who don't remember to use their turn signals, and who can't parallel park.

If the Fall is true, the world should look exactly as it does. We should want what we now want. We should defend what we now defend. We should despise what we now despise. We should feel disgust at every suggestion that such a superstition as sin exists. And we should call every inclination of our hearts good because a distant grandmother long ago decided to become a goddess in defiance of her God.

If we are gods and goddesses, the entire universe must fit into a box small enough for our hands to hold. For example, scientists have now determined the most sexually alluring waist-to-hip ratio for a woman. A materialist will take this information and trace it through the history of natural selection, as if he were working out a piece of long division. He will nail down a conclusion and write a paper for a medical journal explaining why the construction workers on the corner of Fourth and Main hoot at Tilly Johnson every morning as she passes by.

THE DEEP ROMANCE

But while the biologist scratches out the math of enticement, a little old couple in central Ohio shares a hospital bed during visitation hours. The wife has cancer; the husband can hardly see through his cataracts; and yet they are whispering plans for a summer vacation that both of them know will never come. Her breasts have fallen, and all his hair is worn off. Still, he leans over to tell her that she is as beautiful as the day they met—and he means it—and through paper-thin skin, she blushes.

Nothing is gained for the species in this. Not a single improvement in a single chromosome. Yet a golden romance that will never touch our gene pool points to something beyond the material. Talk to me about eagles mating for life or the historical/sociological rationale behind monogamy, and I will listen to you. But deep down, I will also know that none of those stories catches what is really happening between an old couple still in love. No, there's a romance to the universe that can't be reasoned away.

Last night I walked my daughter down a driveway after dark, and she pointed up and said, "There's Cassiopeia."

Either I had forgotten that story or I never knew it—how the wife of Cepheus was beautiful but vain, and how she now floats through the heavens tied to her chair, sometimes holding a mirror, always reminding us of the dangers of pride. I don't think about those old stories enough because now when I look at the stars, I think small thoughts about light-years, and the double-slit experiment, and black holes, and helium gas. I have forgotten how to stand unguarded in the dark and feel small, letting infinity whisper my own vulnerability and longing over me. The Fall resists the undeniable romance of the earth, for romance is dangerous to all that hates the Creator. The Fall is desperate to reduce all the offerings of Eden by pointing to one forbidden handful of fruit, for when Eve took a single bite of sin she lost an entire feast. And when moderns insist on personal divinity, they lose infinitely more than they gain.

How much richer humanity would have been if it had found a way to chase science without shaking all the folktales out of the heavens, for the posture of the storyteller often comes closer to truth than the posture of the materialist. In naming the constellations by rock and flaming gas, we dishonored them most. Likewise, when Nietzsche declared God dead, the eulogy he was truly writing was the eulogy of the human soul. Humanism has not glorified us after all; it has lobotomized us.

T. S. Eliot once wrote,

This is the way the world ends
This is the way the world ends
This is the way the world ends
Not with a bang but a whimper.[9]

Maybe he was right. Perhaps the reign of the *imago Dei* begins to fade before the blue flicker of television on a Thursday night. A thirty-year-old man is watching *Family Guy* reruns on a flat-screen television while his wife scrolls through Facebook. Behold our lesser god and goddess, living to the ends of "My will be done."

Skeptical of Skepticism

As a recovering cynic, I understand why incorporated, modern Christianity has become wearisome to many. I am tired of corruption in the church. I'm tired of big questions answered in small ways. Sometimes I feel alone in the midst of religion gone mad. Some days, I am still stumped by a dead housefly or a rotting deer at the end of my driveway, signs of ugliness and death that make the world feel flat and material. Sometimes I suppress a roar at the seeming injustice of Old Testament laws or the paradoxes that seem to pit James against Romans. I'm not a lemming. I never stop thinking or feeling when I walk in my faith.

But I have also finally (at last) grown old enough to be skeptical of my skepticism. Call me delusional. Call me desperate. But I cannot deny that a metaphysical ache lives inside this animal body—a loneliness for my Creator that pulls me like a migratory bird in the fall.

Yes, I also feel urges to self-rule and self-comfort, but I also feel a deeper pull. I have an instinct to cry out for Narnia and the North. I have the ache of Shasta always knowing somehow that he's not a Calormene.[10] I have the flutter of Lucy, Susan, and Peter when they hear the name of Aslan spoken.

It has been a long and nuanced journey here, sometimes proof-driven and rational, sometimes more mystical. There are parts of my Creator I know with pristine clarity and others I can only see through a glass darkly. While historical and scientific questions about the validity of my faith have mostly been answered through research, other questions remain, keeping me up some nights, tying me in knots others. I yearn for the day when the faith that pulls me onward is transformed to sight.

Yet because I am being taught to rest my epistemology in the living person of Jesus, I am also beginning to see how this strange forge *of process* is being used to reveal the true quality of my heart. I don't see any other reason for an omnipotent being to create the dimension of time other than the provision of a context for human discovery. I used to think of the Christian life as a sort of achievement test in which we were supposed to hurry to figure out all the right answers, but I'm starting to wonder if these slow, hard days of growth help transform us into our eternal form, and therefore are crucial. God lets us live out our belief (and our unbelief) in such a way that the truth of ourselves rises to the surface. Sincere doubt and deflective doubt are divided. What we love most is exposed by our long days of chasing. We are shown ourselves so that we can resign more and more to the indwelling God. Those who love the light pursue the light, and those who love the darkness of self-deification are allowed to feel the gravity of this choice while time remains to make new choices.

I'm also learning that even the darkness of this world is a testimony. Rubble tells us where a bomb was dropped. Miles of scorched mountain land show us the path of a fire. The aftershocks of a great human Fall tremble still. The philosophies of humanism tie "Get Well Soon!" balloons to the rotting legs of our first dead hopes, and the cynic is a vulture who picks apart those carcasses. Yet, all this is exactly how the world should look, if the story of God is true.

Alongside every disaster of human pride, attributes of the holy one also flicker. His threads are woven into the fabric of all disciplines. His sovereignty resounds in the symmetry of the mathematical world. His paradoxes stand in the unreconciled gap between quantum physics and Newtonian physics. Biology teaches us his music. His promises are tucked into the peony. His poetry is written on the back of the barred owl. His mysteries hide with the snapping turtle who sinks down into the black deeps. A choir of fog angels resigns to the morning sun, and I long to obey. I see an old couple holding hands, and I want to be a faithful bride for a holy Bridegroom. He has taught me his paternity by an infant who slept on my chest—milk drunk and heavy with sleep, two little hands folding and unfolding like a sparrow's wings in the moonlight.

The Whisper at Our Backs: A Letter to the Disillusioned

A student knocked on my door. "Mrs. Reynolds, do you have a minute to talk?"

I could tell she was upset, so I pulled up a chair and closed the classroom door to give her space to vent.

"Ever since I can remember," she said, "people have been telling me that the Christian faith is under attack. They warned me about humanists, relativists, evolutionists, globalists, communists, universalists, and liberals. They prepared me for every single argument—but they didn't prepare me for my disappointment in the church.

"I wanted heroes, but I don't admire most of the Christian adults I know. On social media, they forward links to these weird sites—stuff that's almost never legit, if you take time to actually look up the facts. If you try to talk to them in person about what's going on in the world, they don't listen to you. Even if you show them valid research, they interrupt you before you can explain it, calling everything they don't like 'fake news' even if it's undeniably true. They are frantic. Angry. Scared. Their leaders are proud. Their social movements are selfish and hateful.

"Truth doesn't matter to them. It just doesn't. No matter what politicians in their political party have done—they overlook it. All my life, they've told me to be moral—and that's been hard, but I've done it. I haven't slept around. But it doesn't matter that I've held on. I see now that purity means nothing to them. It's just something they tell kids to keep them from getting pregnant."

She was nearly in tears.

"What else?" I asked, wanting to hear it all out before I said anything. Then came the part that really got me.

"You know," she said, "I've thought about this a lot. I would be willing to die for my faith. At least I think I would be; if God is real, he is worth dying for. But watching adults who have lived twenty or thirty years longer than I have act as they are acting right now makes me wonder if this whole Christianity thing is real at all. If older Christians are showing me where this faith is going, I don't want to go with them. I don't want to be on that team."

My heart sank when I heard those words. The faith of this young woman was not being attacked by non-Christians but by immaturity and disobedience in the church of Jesus Christ. For years, I have heard Christian leaders blame the exodus of America's youth on the temptations of the world, but in this student's sharp cry of pain, I heard a different story.

In this letter, I'm going to address disillusionment from several different angles that have been helpful to me during seasons of feeling lost. I'm diversifying because the Bible doesn't give a single, simple solution for weary hearts. Sometimes God shows the disoriented *his plan for justice*, and sometimes he *asks them to confess their own sins*. Sometimes he *tends worn-out bodies and souls with the good stuff of earth*, and sometimes he *reminds the fatigued that he has an intentional plan pulling them back to the soft communion of his voice*. If frustration and disappointment are weighing you down, I don't know what God will use to rejuvenate your heart— but as we work through each of these possibilities, I hope that at least one will hit home. I am asking God to help you feel understood first, then motivated to tackle an old burden with a new perspective.

Restored by Justice

I've prayed so many frustrated prayers the past few years, asking God to silence powerful men who wound the church with hypocrisy and begging him to convict local influences who spread propaganda. I have cried out, "Aren't you ever going to do something to stop them, Lord?" and I've grown impatient with God's silence, and I've even felt a little betrayed by it.

But in my frustration, I've forgotten how tough Jesus promises to be on those who damage the faith of young believers. Once he said,

> But if anyone causes one of these little ones who
> believe in Me to stumble, it would be better for him
> to have a large millstone hung around his neck and
> to be drowned in the depths of the sea. Woe to the
> world for the causes of sin. These stumbling blocks
> must come, but woe to the man through whom
> they come![1]

What if Jesus actually meant this promise? What if people who hurt the faith of a young believer will receive a punishment so severe that it would be better for them to be drowned? That's a sobering warning, and Jesus doesn't sound as if he's joking here. He sounds clear, and he sounds very serious.

As he describes the exact sin of hurting a young believer, Jesus uses an Aramaic term translated to the Greek as σκανδαλίσῃ, a word that connotes blame. It means "to put a snare (in the way), hence to cause to stumble, to give offense."[2] All three of those actions apply to the religious adults who hurt my student's faith. They put a snare in her way, they caused her to stumble in belief, and they gave offense that sowed distrust in her heart. Somehow it helps to realize that Jesus foresaw this sin so clearly. He's not as shocked by our situation as I am. In fact, he's been preparing the church for its own hypocrisy for two thousand years.

I think it's also difficult for me to personalize Christ's promises about false prophets and teachers because those concepts feel so archaic. When I hear "prophet," I think leather sandals, a flax tunic, and a wild beard. It takes work to remember that the false prophets of our era are more likely to show up in boat shoes and Brooks Brothers. They will be alert and articulate men who know what's on our news—men who understand how we feel about legitimate cultural concerns like abortion, and health insurance, and immigration. But not only will they know how we *feel* about those issues, they will know *how to maneuver us* by what we fear and what we desire. They will use good causes to lead us to bad behavior and bad beliefs.

These men might show up as televangelists who steal money from lonely old women living off Social Security. More likely, though, the false prophets of our time will embed themselves inside the causes and institutions we trust. Because we love our families, a false prophet will create fear-and-shame-based parenting programs that promise to keep our children safe. If we love our nation, they will show up as pastors who make unholy alliances with political figures. Modern false prophets won't be fringe leaders with wild hair and wild eyes because outliers don't collect large followings very often. They will know that it's far more effective to derail a moving train than it is to build one from scratch.

The Bible tells us that false prophets will project a fabricated godliness, a corruption of religion that will imitate goodness while bearing none of the gospel's true power (see

2 Timothy 3:5). While following them, the religious public will not hold to sound doctrine. Instead, it will organize a huge network of false pastors, men whose words and promises tickle the ears of the masses (see 2 Timothy 4:3). Is this prospect haunting? Have you thought that the greatest threats to the church would come only from outside her walls? I once did too, but I wasn't listening to what the Bible actually says. In fact, the Word tells us that certain religious leaders will abandon the truth for myths, and that masses of people will follow along, using a distortion of religion to confirm their preexisting biases.

At present, strange forces within Christianity are attempting to vivisect the gospel into isolated, stand-alone virtues instead of reaching continually for the indwelling person of Christ. This causes a small piece of something good to be used for harm. As Chesterton once wrote,

> The modern world is not evil; in some ways the modern world is far too good. It is full of wild and wasted virtues. When a religious scheme is shattered (as Christianity was shattered at the Reformation), it is not merely the vices that are let loose. The vices are, indeed, let loose, and they wander and do damage. But the virtues are let loose also; and the virtues wander more wildly, and the virtues do more terrible damage. *The modern world is full of the old Christian virtues gone mad. The virtues have gone*

*mad because they have been isolated from each other
and are wandering alone.*[3]

What is our modern world but a raging roar of virtues?
No matter what our denomination, or political affiliation, or
perspective on the world, we collect into self-righteous mobs
and rant. We stare at former friends like citizens of Babel,
realizing that we no longer speak the same language. "It's
crazy out there," we whisper to the few we trust.

"We may say that the most characteristic current philosophies have not only a touch of mania, but a touch of sui-
cidal mania," Chesterton wrote,[4] and too much of religious
America has adopted a kamikaze mission. We sacrifice the
war for the sake of our pet battles, and in the wake of this
frenzy, the "little ones" Christ loves have grown wounded
and disheartened. Eighteen-year-olds who wanted a God
worth dying for are wandering off into the wilderness grieving. The fairy tale of the gospel seems like smoke and mirrors
to them now.

What will happen to those leaders who hurt young believers this way? I'm not completely sure. I do know that in
some of the sternest language he ever uses, Jesus says that
not everyone who calls him "Lord" will enter the Kingdom.
He's not negating faith-based salvation here; he's clarifying
it—*religious language doesn't equal religious reality.* Even those
who direct ministries, completing long lives of religious service, may be cast away from him. Though these words are
stern, despair lifts from my heart when I remember that God

promises to deal with false teachers. I don't have to carry the weight of the whole religious machine on my shoulders. Even if he's silent right now, ultimately, he's got this.

I'm also encouraged to realize how gently he speaks about those people who are harmed by bad religious leadership. He calls those who stumble *little ones* (μικρῶν) in Matthew 18[5]— a version of the same word Jesus uses when he says that anyone who gives one of these "little ones" a drink in his name will not lose his reward.[6] This also stems from the same root word Jesus uses to say that the angels of the "little ones" always behold the face of the Father,[7] the same root word used when God doesn't want one of the "little ones" to perish,[8] the same root word used when he says, "Fear not, little flock" in Luke.[9]

When we grow disillusioned and overwhelmed by the impact of false teachers in our culture, seeing God's plan for justice can restore our courage. The Bible predicted the spiritual chaos of our time—in fact, our quasi-evangelical dialogue was foretold with laser precision. He has always known that it would come to this, and he is ready.

Restored by Confession

Even as the words of Jesus help me come to peace with the sins of others, they also convict me of my own recklessness, driving me to repentance. Repentance might seem like a strange remedy for disillusionment, but in some situations, it can actually be one of the most effective because we don't always realize how unconfessed sin is weighing our hearts down.

In particular, Twitter is my rage candy. Whenever I'm incensed with the latest political debacle, I can tag any charlatan in America and blast away at him. I don't mean to imply that exhortation is always out of place—sometimes a stern word is fitting. It's important to call out evil where it has taken root. But too often, I don't fight in the Spirit. Too often, I fight in disgust, in disappointment, in cynicism— operating entirely out of my own power. The Lord will usually let me run a while on this leash, but after an hour or two, I'm exhausted. *Why do I feel so awful?* I wonder. Well, because the greatest battles of this world weren't meant to be conquered by human effort.

It's sobering to realize that those people who caused my student to stumble believed they were fighting the good fight. They saw how progressive theology and politics stood poised to take over America, and they wanted to help resist those threats. What they failed to remember, however—what I fail to remember—is that standing against a flawed force isn't the same thing as walking in dependence upon the Spirit to accomplish good. In fact, the temptation to fight in human strength is a diversion tactic from our enemy. He knows how much harm we can do by taking matters into our own hands. In the book of Revelation, Jesus corrects the church at Ephesus by saying,

Without growing weary, you have persevered and
endured many things for the sake of My name. But
I have this against you: You have abandoned your

first love. Therefore, keep in mind how far you have fallen. Repent and perform the deeds you did at first.[10]

If these verses are correct, it's possible to work for the cause of Jesus while losing sight of why we started fighting in the first place. A religious or political endeavor that begins with all the best intentions can spin wildly off course. If Satan can't get us to deny Christ, he will try to twist our vision. He will try to destroy the good we want to do by calcifying our extremes. Victor Hugo nailed this danger in his epic tome *Les Misérables*:

> *To be Ultra is to go one better.* It is to attack the
> scepter in the name of the throne and the miter
> in the name of the altar; it is to maltreat the thing
> you trundle around; it is to kick over the traces;
> it is to quibble with the stake over the degree of
> cooking required for heretics; it is to attack the idol
> for lacking in idolatry; to insult through excessive
> respect; to find too little popery in the pope, too
> little royalty in the king, and too much light in
> night; it is to find alabaster, snow, the swan, and the
> lily sadly wanting when it comes to whiteness; *to
> support things in a partisan spirit to the point where
> you become their enemy; it is to be so strongly for that
> you are against.*[11]

In the past ten years, we've seen a rash of dystopian books and movies (*The Hunger Games*, zombie flicks, etc.) in which humans devolve into savages. I think these plots are on the rise because our barbaric culture makes us feel as if we are all fading to animal form. In the conscious daylight, we run confident and free, but at night, secularism haunts our subconscious and feeds our narrative nightmares. The scientists tell us we are nothing but beasts. Then what will become of us? Will we devour one another, then be devoured, then turn to dust?

But there is far more to the story than this. Confession and repentance are always available to the believer in Christ. We don't have to let the darkness of our time choke out our light. If we have had a beastly day, or a beastly week, or a beastly year, we can run to the Lord and admit our failures. He will forgive us for whatever has driven us to reactivity and help us live an indwelt life instead. Yes, it's tough to be a believer right now, but Christians living in a complex, post-Christian culture like ours can also grow from the threats of our time. Just as weight lifting improves the density of bones, the gravity of the modern era can solidify our faith.

I don't mean our struggle will be painless or easy, but as we learn our own weaknesses, confess them, and learn to walk more closely with Jesus, Christians (like my student) will eventually become stronger in these confusing times, not weaker. We can grow like Corrie ten Boom, a woman who asked hard questions, then emerged with more reliance upon God's voice, more trust in his heart, more patience, more focus, and more hope. "In darkness God's truth shines most clear," she said.[12] She learned to see truly through trial, and so can we.

Restored by Memories and Open Air

The first time I read chapter 13 of *The Screwtape Letters*, I was shocked by what Lewis seemed to be suggesting. In this chapter, a human is saved from damnation by taking a simple walk in open air. Before this walk, the human was hanging out in crowded places with proud friends who flattered and distracted him. However, the act of getting outdoors in a familiar landscape clears his mind and renovates his vision. Exposure to nature undermines the plans of evil, refreshing the man's courage and faith.

The mentor demon named Screwtape lambasts his protégé (Wormwood) for letting the human go "down to the old mill and have tea there—a walk through country he really likes, and taken alone."[13] Screwtape is an experienced tempter who understands the importance of the rhythms of everyday life, those natural and humble joys that "kill by contrast all the trumpery" the demons "have been so laboriously teaching him to value."[14]

Until reading this chapter in *The Screwtape Letters*, I never considered a change of environment seriously. Going to the beach. Getting out of town. A hike in the woods. Those things usually made me *feel* better, but I didn't think about the possibility that God was very much involved in such a method of restoration. Like those Gnostic heretics who divided the stuff of the spirit from the stuff of the body, I had assigned a hierarchy to my human parts. My spirit could help my body, but never vice versa.

But as I consider the disillusionment of our time, it's interesting to take note of what most of us do with our bodies over the course of the day. We sit very still in our rooms, staring into digital screens. We scroll through disturbing headlines for hours. Our heart rates increase. Our hope fades. Our anger swells. We sabotage our peace and trust by gravitating toward chaos and disaster. This bodily behavior impacts our thought processes, and it impacts our faith.

Jesus was a model of breaking away from the masses to spend time alone outdoors. So often in the Bible, we find him stealing off under big skies to walk and pray. He put legs on his fatigue. I think we should follow his lead on that.

I also think we need to consider the potential power of our own memories. In one of my favorite children's books,[15] a little field mouse named Frederick collects beauty for winter. During harvest months, all the busy mice scoff at Frederick for gathering memories instead of food, but when the bitterness of the long cold threatens weary hearts as well as bodies, Frederick pulls out his stories to revive the community.

We see a similar principle throughout the Bible. Over and again, memories of God's faithfulness are used to lead discouraged hearts onward and upward. In 1 Samuel 7:12, Samuel names a stone Ebenezer as a visual reminder of God's faithfulness. In Psalm 77, Asaph counteracts his own despair by recounting the past deeds of God. A simple search for the word *remember* brings up dozens of examples of God's attempts to reorient his people through past stories of his work in their lives.

About a year ago, I started setting a kitchen timer to half-hour intervals, little pockets of time devoted to writing down memories. I didn't think of this as a spiritual exercise at the time—I was just feeling homesick for the simplicity of my past. The details that surfaced as I wrote surprised me, but I was even more surprised to realize how I felt as I returned to all these different times and places. So many long, slow hours. So much comfort. How was life ever like this? At the end of those writing sessions, I felt less captive, less distressed, more humane.

My initial bursts of writing were done recklessly, intent on collecting impressions only. But when I returned to those images reflectively, seeking to look deeper into what I remembered, I realized that they were full of lessons that I had internalized subconsciously. So many events that felt like normal life were actually training my heart. So many details that seemed peripheral were formative. In even the simplest moment of my childhood, I could tell that God had been training me—not with exegesis but by narrative.

I'll show you what I mean in this next section, italicizing those lessons I internalized three decades before I could verbalize them.[16] Maybe you can glance over my journey and then be inspired to take a walk back through your own formative moments as a result.

My Reflections

I was born to the sort of people who know where the wall-eye hide and how to keep tomatoes alive in a drought year. Pappaw liked to make jokes, eat Fritos, and play Rook. On Saturdays his whiskers scratched, but come Sunday, he was smooth as a deacon. When I kissed him, he smelled like Aqua Velva, and I was proud of him.

Mammaw had the prettiest silver hair, and she'd curl it until it made a soft cloud around her face. Her youth still fluttered in her eyelashes, and she wore shirtwaist dresses that showed what time and maternity had done to her body. *I didn't know what the world expected of women back then, so I didn't see sags or weight. I thought she was beautiful.*

Their back porch held hooks for camo jackets hung five or six deep. Every time I'd walk in, I'd take a big, deep breath because I loved the smell of bluegill, and rain, and tractor oil, and work boots. A line of wooden birdcalls hung from leather strings, and we cousins would blow them until our lips went numb from the vibrations. Shotguns and rifles were all over the place, but kids were taken out into a field and shown what a gun could do. From an early age, *we were taught that humans were powerful creators, capable of hurting other humans, and that we were responsible for our actions.*

When I was taught how to pull skin off a squirrel and pick buckshot out of his meat with my fingers, I began to understand death differently. Splitting the squirrel's belly, I found the organs that were supposedly in my own body: a tiny liver, a heart, intestines, still warm and full from life. Hours later, I would lie in my bed and push on the soft part of my belly, looking for those same parts, rolling my mortality around in my mind. *I could tell that my body was a fragile thing. I was dust, and to dust I would return, and that made me want to live life carefully.*

When I first saw the limp neck of a beautiful ten-point buck on his way to the butcher, I grieved. That same morning, this powerful being had stood erect and free as any buck I had ever seen on the edge of a wood, but now it was dead weight. He was dead as Lazarus—Lazarus, whose cold neck would have flopped and bobbled like this while his sisters watched men carry him into the tomb. My friend, the professor of veterinary medicine, says biology alone can't explain the loss of life's spark in an animal. Sometimes a little dog can have all the parts it needs to live, and yet it is not alive, nor can it be made alive. In the weight of a dead buck, I realized what a wild thing it was for Jesus to take an empty body and make it alive again. *Life was fragile, but Christ was mighty.*

When we were in copperhead territory, Pappaw carried his pistol on his hip. We lived relaxed but ready. Even before I knew that Nehemiah's people carried swords while rebuilding Jerusalem,[17] good men carrying weapons taught me to expect a world fraught with hidden dangers, showed me that even on the most lighthearted of expeditions, I needed to stay alert for an enemy who strikes out of nowhere. *Learning to scan tall grass, I gained a metaphor for an enemy who prowls around waiting for us. I began to see why a spiritual wilderness must always be met with the weapons of a shrewd faith (see Ephesians 6:10-20).*

Christmas dinners at Mammaw and Pappaw's, the men wore white V-neck T-shirts with their chest hairs curling at the collars. We gave one another University of Kentucky sweatshirts and long gray utility socks. We read Luke 2 from that heavy old Bible while the children wiggled, then we sank into old couches and sagging blue recliners, sticking our bare toes and fingers through holes in yarn blankets, sitting close together and making up time.

Mammaw Kelley sat me down most summers with a real stretched canvas, professional paintbrushes, linseed oil, and oil paints. She wasn't afraid I would ruin her expensive supplies; instead, she handed over the best of the best and trusted me. Oil paint lets you paint over and over until you get the thing right, and that's how things were at Mammaw Kelley's house. It didn't matter what you'd messed up—your first painting of a chickadee, or your teenage years, or your faith—she loved you, forgave you, and trusted you to make a better go of it next time. She knew that growth takes time. *The Lord is slow to anger and abounding in love,*[18] *and when I hear those verses, I think about how much I could have confessed to my grandmother without her even flinching.* "You learned something," she would say. "You don't like how that went. You'll grow from that."

Every Christmas, the walls were full of art. There were paintings of daisies, and three brown wrens, and wooden barns falling down, and deer standing solemnly in moon-light. It was low art, I suppose, but it was the stuff of our everyday life. When I went to college on an art scholarship and learned what educated people expected of beauty, I was embarrassed to have loved so many of the wrong things, but I've learned since that there are worse aesthetic sins to commit than the sins of the rural eye. *The mortal sins of art—like the mortal sins of all humankind—are pride and cynicism.* There is not nearly so much wrong with two happy wrens painted on a circular saw blade as there is with a painting of a withered, blank-eyed woman staring out of an apartment window into a flat, gray world. The former may be sentimental, but the latter is a sacrilege.

Our Christmas tree was always cedar, and it stood a ways from the wood-burning stove. I pulled the bagworms off the branches and threw them in the fire, where they'd pop. That stove was always ten degrees too hot because Pappaw had known what it meant to be cold. So we sweated and were thankful when classy Aunt Reba showed up in her fitted tweed jacket, blasting a line of winter among us.

In the bathroom, there was a vinyl toilet seat covered in blue foam. It stuck to your backside and sighed when you sat. Mammaw kept her diary in the second bathroom drawer from the right. I read it once when I was old enough to know better than to read other people's private things, but in those pages, I saw how she prayed for me when nobody was watching but Jesus. The book of Hebrews tells us that our faith falls into a line of a great cloud of witnesses, saints who have come before us—men and women of whom the world was not worthy. But I first learned about my spiritual lineage while swinging my legs on a sticky blue toilet seat, reading the prayers of my grandmother for my life. At seven, that didn't mean much to me, but there have been days in the past ten years when I've held on to that memory like a lifeline.

I slept in the room where my dad had slept as a boy, picking sand from the sandpile off my scalp with my fingernails. The four walls were blond wood paneling, and there were medals from track meets hanging in a shadow box. The blankets smelled a little like fried potatoes. When I couldn't sleep, I pulled back the thin white bedroom curtain and looked out into the yard where the horizon was stripped down to lines. The trees were calligraphic, inking messages I couldn't translate, and the lights of the nearby coal mine were yellow, running down a slant into the earth while the natural gas pumps genuflected, even on Christmas Day. The fields were frozen. I could tell they would crunch under my shoes.

I watched all this for a good while, feeling something I couldn't quite name.

For unto you is born this day a Savior,
    who is Christ the Lord.[19]

I had learned those lines in the third grade, the revelry of an angel bringing good news to people like mine. Country people. Shepherds. Simple folks who could receive the gospel with joy instead of cynicism. The richest members of society have always had precious little chance of getting through the eye of the needle of God's company—Jesus said that way was narrow and that few would find it. *"You will seek me and find me when you seek me with all your heart."*[20] *It's a test that boils down to posture.*

An Embodied Faith

In *Desiring the Kingdom*, James K. A. Smith suggested that humans don't interact with the world primarily through cognition or perception but through our loves.[21] What we care about, what we actually chase as we live day to day, can make a big impact on what we become.

Because we chase what we love, the stories that define our lives matter a great deal. I don't mean that there is anything mystical about a narrative. I do mean that our experiences and our affections influence our defaults. If you have ever tried to will yourself into losing twenty pounds, you know how rarely that works; but if you fall in love with jujitsu, or swimming, or distance running, that weight might easily disappear as you chase a greater delight.

Smith wrote, "It's not so much that we're intellectually convinced and then muster the willpower to pursue what we ought; rather, at a precognitive level, we are attracted to a vision of the good life that has been painted for us in stories and myths, images and icons. It is not primarily our minds that are captivated but rather our *imaginations* that are captured, and when our imagination is hooked, *we're* hooked."[22]

Jesus knew this about us. When he was speaking to fishermen, he explained the vision of the Kingdom by using the stories of their world. ("See how your nets break? Come be fishers of men.")[23] He told parable after parable, stories about a lost coin, and a lost sheep, and a lost son. Often, he spoke in visual metaphors. "I am the bread of life."[24] "I am the light of the world."[25] These are the sorts of images that take root. Sometimes he explained those stories. Sometimes he just let them soak. As he works all things in our complex lives together according to his will, I think sometimes he still does the same.

Physical actions like walking and writing can become weirdly mystical if you take them out of context. When used properly, however, they can be used by God to encourage our weary souls. They can acknowledge the wholeness of our humanity and nourish us affectively instead of just cognitively.

Do you remember when the prophet Elijah was running from Ahab and Jezebel before he finally collapsed exhausted in the desert? The angel of the Lord let the poor guy sleep, and then he woke him up twice to give him food, saying, "Get up and eat, or else you'll get too tired to travel." After Elijah ate, the Bible says, "The food and water made him strong enough to walk forty more days."[26] Did you get that? The food and water made him strong enough. Not prayer. Not a leap of faith. Physical nourishment.

I've always loved that simple story because it shows me how God understands the bodily and emotional needs of the weary.

It would have been easy enough for the Lord to zap Elijah with supernatural power to complete the journey. Instead, he let him experience sleep and food, a restoration built from the plain stuff of earth. Restoration by memory, by vision, and by open skies can provide a similar sort of healing from the Father. For me, this restoration often comes through writing, but if writing isn't your thing, or if most of your memories are still too painful for you to rehearse, try Lewis's suggestion and spend thirty minutes out in the open air. Shut the laptop. Turn off the phone. Get outside, and move, and breathe. You might be surprised by what the Lord reveals to you as you go.

Restored by an Assignment

"I wish it need not have happened in my time," said Frodo.

"So do I," said Gandalf, "and so do all who live to see such times. But that is not for them to decide. All we have to decide is what to do with the time that is given us."[27]

I've returned to those beloved lines from Tolkien's *The Fellowship of the Ring* a hundred times this past year. They seem to ring out in harmony with Ephesians 2:10, a verse that tells us how God made us by hand (in Jesus) for good works that he prepared long ago for these very days we are living.

As I sit in my bedroom floor editing this chapter, my back aching after two twelve-hour shifts at revision, my eyes burning, my heart exhausted, my soul fed up with the news, my spirit irritated with evangelical corruption, ready to throw this whole book in the trash and run away to some cabin in the woods with a stack of Russian novels, I'm shocked to see that reminder sitting on my own page. *I was made by hand for specific works that God prepared for me to do. Yeah, I'm tired as all get-out, but it's going to be okay. Jesus is here. He's going to show me what to do next.*

Sometimes we feel as overwhelmed as two squatty little hobbits trying to carry a magic ring to Mordor, a task that is too difficult to bear. Or we feel like Odysseus trying to sail between Scylla and Charybdis; our journey feels doomed. We're going to either be eaten by a terrible six-headed monster or get sucked down to a whirlpool of death. We watch epic movies with dark lords, dragons, and mountains full of fire, and we can tell that somehow we got swept up into a quest just as daunting. But being here feels wrong. We're out of place. People like us are better at sitting in taverns in the Shire while somebody else faces up to Sauron.

"I don't want to do this. I wish I didn't have to be here." I've prayed this more than once. Maybe you have too. But courage can come in the reminder that today is a little pocket of time that's being given to us. Our assignments have been prepared for us ahead of time. We don't have to do the impossible. We just have to listen to the voice of our Shepherd moment by moment.

Restored by Union

Two of my friends wait each day now in a hospice facility, sitting beside the bed of their teenage daughter. They are so brave, and they are so tired. Emma was in a coma-like state for months, and though she is experiencing some progress at last (praise God!), that progress is happening too slowly for all of us who love her. We wanted her out of bed yesterday, laughing and jabbering again. My fingers tremble as I write those words for you because Emma is one of my favorite students, a ball of fire, mischief, and laughter. She loves C. S. Lewis, and being outside, and she has a sharp, dry wit.

When I visited her in the hospital, I tried to pray with her mom and dad in the cafeteria, but after I got to "Dear Lord," I couldn't make any more words. My heart suddenly flooded over with grief, and I put my head down on the table and wept. Her mom and dad were kind to me, and we held hands while I tried to get my breath. Nobody should ever have to do any of this for a nineteen-year-old.

"Isaiah 30:21," her father said gently. "And your ears shall hear a word behind you, saying, 'This is the way, walk in it,' when you turn to the right or when you turn to the left." Then he said, "In all of this terrible time, the Lord has shown us so far which steps to take. He's always told us where to turn. Pray that the whisper remains."

"Tomorrow is one day. We take one day at a time," said her mother.

When I walked into the parking lot, I felt as if a hard piece of square plastic were shoved down in my throat. I've never felt grief so tactile. I had kept my composure bedside, just in case Emma could hear me, but in the cafeteria, and then in the open air, my knees felt as if they would collapse.

Yet Emma's father was right, and I've thought about his words often since he said them to me. There are so many parts of my world that aren't healing as quickly as I wanted them to. My country is hurting. My family is hurting. The church I love is hurting. Some nights, I feel despair because so much is so broken.

But even in the dark, I can wait for the voice of Christ saying, "Step here. Step here." I can know that his leading will come because this is the time that has been given to me. He has already provided strong memories to undergird me. He has provided open skies and deep forests full of running water. He has provided good, long paths to walk, lungs to take in morning air, blood that grows delightfully warm with exertion. I have been given bread, and water, and sleep. I have been given honest friends to remind me of truth that I forget.

The Lord sees every bit of corruption that strains my hope, and he feels deep, paternal compassion for those who are wounded by bad leaders. He's promised to deal sternly with men and women who never repent from proud and selfish dominance while also offering to forgive all who run to him confessing that we've been sucked into the madness. Yes, these are stern times, but lo, he is with us always. The cultural battle may not look quite like we once thought it would, but this is still God's ordained classroom for us, a place where we will learn to hear, trust, and follow him.

Martin Luther once wrote, "And though this world, with devils filled, Should threaten to undo us, We will not fear, for

God hath willed His truth to triumph through us."[28] Luther could have written these words for years as devilishly strange as ours, but that doesn't mean all is lost. God will triumph through us because Jesus is close. Every morning, every evening, he will lead us on.

Not All Who Wander Are Lost: A Letter to the Expat

Last summer I visited an Amish greenhouse with my parents. It's so far back, there's no easy way to get there. You have to wind past the rock quarry, drive beyond the fields of yellow canola, take a right by the aluminum mailbox, and follow a long, crackling gravel driveway until it divides a two-story farmhouse from three round-top tents.

You'll know you've made it when you have to slow down for an eight-year-old boy who uses that same driveway for the family horse wagon. The animal is strong-shouldered but compliant to a gentle command. The boy wears a straw hat with a wide brim, and the soles of his little bare feet are black and thick from outdoor wear. He keeps his balance by pushing his arches into the singletree, which leaves his toes free to bounce according to the jostle of the lane.

A girl of about fifteen with short, dirty fingernails, no makeup, and flushed pink cheeks works the greenhouse cash register. The front of her navy cotton dress doesn't have any buttons. She keeps it together by a line of straight sewing pins, somehow managing not to snag her arms on their sharp tips, hard as she labors.

Her mother tends the same tent, and all around her is the scent of lavender and lemon thyme, along with the smell of a human body working. That smell doesn't bother me, and it never has. It reminds me of old people from my childhood—the wiry sort who wore long cotton shirtsleeves in August and kept their shirttails tucked in day and night.

Mom told me that the Amish greenhouse is offering a new product this year: little fairy gardens, baskets full of succulents and tiny figurines. I say "fairy garden," but that's not quite right. There are no dragons, elves, wizards, or fairies—just tiny replicas of everyday farm life in miniature. One basket has a two-inch clothesline, and another a wooden bench the size of a paper clip. There is a well (for drawing water, not wishes) and a one-room church building.

When I ask the teenage girl if she has fun deciding what should go into each scene, her eyes light up, and she flushes even pinker. So many young women her age have learned to be vain, silly, and severe, but her innocence reminds me of an old Shaker song that I have always loved:

'Tis the gift to be simple, 'tis the gift to be free
'Tis the gift to come down where we ought to be,
And when we find ourselves in the place just right,
'Twill be in the valley of love and delight.

When true simplicity is gain'd,
To bow and to bend we shan't be asham'd,
To turn, turn will be our delight,
Till by turning, turning we come 'round right.[1]

I feel a twinge of something almost like jealousy as we drive away. Living close to the earth, by hard physical labor and by humble faith, is breathtaking work in a frantic culture like ours. Though my theology differs from that of the Amish, it is riveting to witness the beauty of people who live slowly. Their lives feel almost like a biosphere, a pocket of civility in the corner of a global cage fight.

If you are coming to this letter in the middle of a long and confusing journey, you probably long for a chance to breathe like that. Maybe your seven-year dating relationship broke down, or your career crashed as you were hitting peak performance. Maybe after decades of prayers, your adult child still can't seem to get his act together. Maybe there's a general sense of futility to everything right now—a feeling of meaninglessness in which the past seems dull and the future seems unclear. Maybe, as Bilbo Baggins once said, you feel thin and stretched like "butter that has been scraped over too much bread."[2] In this book, we've already addressed several clear points of pain—we've talked about precise sorrows like abuse and rejection and chaos. But there's also a different sort of struggle that comes in the foggy funk of life, in years that refuse to snap immediately into place within a grand and beautiful narrative.

In the midst of this kind of weariness, we may be tempted to romanticize the lives of the Amish, tempted to withdraw from all that is weighing us down. But finding simplicity isn't the primary purpose of human existence, and God isn't limited to years that look ideal. Communion with him can also be found in rooms that feel foreign, in the real struggles that rise in savage environments; in fact, our time in the underworld of meaninglessness can offer a special sort of sanctuary—an opportunity to make mass inside the mess.

God in All Places

My hometown was the seat of the first diocese west of the Appalachian Mountains, established in 1808 by Pope Pius VII. Until 1841, our diocese ministered to Catholics between the Appalachian Mountains and the Mississippi River. In many areas of the South, Catholicism is shunned, but where I grew up, it was revered. Tourists would come from all over the world to visit our cathedral.

As a Southern Baptist, I was accustomed to strong emotions, potluck dinners, and lots of hugs. "The priesthood of the believer" was more than just a doctrine—it was a way of life. We were congregation-led and democratic. Sunday school classes left room for debate, and because we felt personally responsible for guarding and giving the truth, we opened our Bibles and wrestled over nuance. This was the world I knew—the faith I knew—so when my parents enrolled me in a local Catholic school as a seventh grader, I had no idea what to expect.

The first time I attended mass at St. Joseph's Basilica, I was overwhelmed. The vaulted ceilings seemed to lift my soul up and out of my body like a balloon full of helium. Even before my classmates began to kneel and genuflect, I felt a compulsion to fall to my knees. I wondered if we entered the cathedral in silent reverence to keep us all from shouting out in awe.

So much was foreign to me there—the stations of the cross, the holy water that first dripped and then clung to the fingertips of my friends, the statue of a kind-eyed saint I did not know, the recitations. "Lamb of God, take away the sins of the world. Lamb of God, take away the sins of the world. Lamb of God, take away the sins of the world. Have mercy on us." The artwork on the walls was holy, serious, and dark, but my heart pounded with delight when I realized that people here made no apologies for mystery. When the ancient songs were sung, I felt as if I had wandered into Lothlórien or some other enchanted world. As a Protestant, I didn't align with every aspect of Catholic theology, but there were also elements of mass that I realized I needed.

During those years, I grew close to a nun and a priest. Father Bill would dress up like a clown, red nose and all. He was different from a pastor; his focus was singular, undivided by family demands. I loved his levity and his humility.

Then there was Sister Theresa. She was maybe four foot nine, Italian, and fierce. On days the boys were terrible, she'd let out a string of foreign words that I was glad I couldn't understand. Once I saw her throw a hardback grammar book at a kid named Doug. With me, though, she was gentle. She asked me what I believed during catechism class, knowing that I was Southern Baptist. When my classmates dared to giggle, she told them sternly that Baptists knew how to study their Bibles and that Catholics had a lot to learn from them. When it was her turn to talk, she told us all stories of saints and miracles, stories that delighted me, even if I didn't fully believe all of them.

Every day at lunch, Sister Theresa would eat half a grapefruit with a spoon that had a jagged blade on one side. I would watch her work out the sections, worried that she would cut herself to pieces. But she was old, agile, and unafraid. She let me section out my doctrine with a blade too. She relaxed around me, creating a barrier of protection around our dialogue, and I loved her for it.

In this dear Catholic school, I learned to play basketball. I was a moderate little player, not squirrely enough to play point guard, and not tall enough to play center. But I made a solid forward, and I could play second guard in a pinch. My biggest strength was that I hustled. Every single game, I gave it all I had. The same love and support that filled our catechism classes ruled our court. Coaches corrected us and believed in us, insisting on good sportsmanship. We learned to cheer for one another and reach a hand to our enemies when they fell.

But in ninth grade, I switched to the big county school, and county was a different planet. I saw bloody fights in the hallway, and there was a constant reek of pot and stale denim. A combined smoking area welcomed both teachers and students; through a glass door, I saw them together in a nicotine fog between class bells. Field parties roared on the weekends, but starting Monday, apathy ruled. It was a world of Metallica, giant mullets, and black eyeliner. I didn't know the cadence. I didn't know the vernacular.

I was fourteen when I walked into the county gym for my first day of high-school basketball camp. Switching from a small private school to a huge public school was terrifying, so I had stayed up late the night before, weaving colored ribbons through two metal hair barrettes. Red, white, and blue—the team colors. I wore those to practice because I wanted to let the natives know that I was friendly.

As I walked to the bleachers, I saw high-school girls who moved like the boys I had always known, throwing themselves at hard angles between steps. Their jaws were clenched, and several of them kept a sort of permanent snarl on their faces. I had seen television shows with rough street gangs, but the saunter, the taunt, the threat, the dare—I had never seen any of this in a living female.

Earlier that summer I had practiced walking up and down underneath the long tunnel of catalpa trees, my head up and my shoulders back, learning to plant my heels so that they came down softly and with dignity. Nearly every toddler learns to walk, of course, but as a child becomes a woman, her weight begins to collect in different places, so she has to learn to walk a second time. If she doesn't, she won't know how to hold her chest or her hips; she will let her breasts fold in, and she will bend over and sort of clunk along. I wanted to float, so balancing a thick novel on my head, I had walked back and forth under those trees, squishing the black-and-yellow catalpa worms that fell en masse onto the asphalt below.

Even though I was scared to walk into that high-school gym, I remembered the grace I had practiced, held my head up, and held my shoulders back.

"Get them ***** ribbons outta your hair, Princess," one of the seniors barked.

"I don't know what kind of ***** world you come from," said another, "but this is serious ball here at the county, and the next time I see you wearing ***** ribbons like that, I'm gonna rip them out myself."

Apparently, the upperclassmen held some sort of authority. The other freshmen laughed as I scrambled with the clips. "***** rich private-school kid," I heard somebody whisper.

The other seniors glowered. The freshmen went silent, looking around nervously to see what they should do next, then setting their jaws in a clench.

When one of the coaches walked in, I saw something in his eyes I haven't seen in many people since. It felt like a liquid hatred, the sort of hatred that thinks it's doing you a favor by despising you. On bus trips, if we hadn't performed well in a game, he would stand at the front, arms on two seats, swaying back and forth with the motion of the bus, and pointing out girls one at a time. He would say, "Thomas, I know your momma. I know your daddy. I know what kind of ***** they are. And you played like ***** tonight because you came from a ***** family, and unless you get your ***** together, you're always going to be ***** just like your ***** people."

I'd never heard an adult talk like that in my whole life. I looked down at my knees, hoping he wouldn't notice me.

One by one he worked through us, berating us, trying to figure out what would hurt us the most. I will never forget the first time he addressed me: "You wish you were back at that prep school, don't you." (It wasn't a question.) "All those rich folks baby their precious kids—well, you're not precious here. You're nothing here."

My parents weren't rich. We didn't even go to restaurants. I didn't tell him. I didn't say anything but "Yes, sir." None of us ever said anything but "Yes, sir. No, sir."

Some of my first exposures to sexual talk were among this crowd. In the locker rooms, the girls would laugh in smoky, harsh voices, telling stories about man bodies while they pulled up their knee socks and tightened their high-tops. For them, sex was about conquest, about exposing men as fools. Sex was power—something that gave teenage girls the right to call grown men by their first names.

The apostle Paul once said, "I want you to be wise as to what is good and innocent as to what is evil,"[3] but I didn't know how to be innocent there. To be naive was to be slaughtered. I learned how to cuss, learned how to throw an elbow, learned how to deflect attack with a cold stare. I learned how to stop acting as if I cared because caring was weakness, and predators smell blood in the water from miles off.

I felt terrible about who I was becoming, but I wasn't sure how to survive any other way. "God, if you want me to be innocent, why did you leave me here where innocence is impossible?" I prayed. Day and night, I felt guilty. Day and night, I felt trapped. But looking back on those years, I wonder if God was allowing me to see my own limitations. In fact, maybe showing me *what I couldn't do* was even more important to him than moving me into an environment where it would have been easier to behave in the power of my own strength.

The Importance of Time in the Underworld
When We Find Our Underworld

Joseph Campbell is not my favorite literary critic, but his "Hero's Journey" story model provides a helpful illustration for the dark times of our lives. Campbell explains that in many epics, a protagonist travels down into some sort of underworld where he faces dangers that threaten to undo him. As he survives those dangers, he emerges back in the upperworld with a boon to offer humanity.

My high-school years were an underworld, a terrible season of losing my orientation and losing myself. But in that chaos, I began to grasp my need for a gospel that could be carried to the darkness. If I had been able to jump through every religious hoop perfectly when I was a teenager, I would have stepped into adulthood with an inaccurate picture of my own righteousness. I would have claimed to love Jesus, but I wouldn't have known how much I actually needed him. In fact, I might have thought that I was doing him a favor by standing up for him. Instead, during those four years, I saw what darkness I was capable of chasing. I learned that I didn't just have a Savior to offer the world—I stood in profound need of him too.

Jesus prayed to his Father, "I do not ask that you take them out of the world, but that you keep them from the evil one,"[4] and this can be a frustrating verse for those of us who want to cloister our children and ourselves. I'm drawn to protected microcosms because I think I might make fewer mistakes there. I'm that guy from the Bible who wants to bury his talents in the earth instead of investing them because he's scared of losing what he's been given. I want to lower my risks and end up breaking even.

Jesus, on the other hand, seems to want us to carry the ring to Mordor against all odds of our own flesh and nature, and you can't take a journey like that without losing all delusions of your own grandeur. While walking through the world, you're going to find your ugliest weaknesses. You're going to realize that your flesh is sometimes greedy, sometimes false, sometimes dishonest, and often weary. But in the limits of our ability, by our weaknesses and our failures, we learn to cry out to God in a whole different way. We learn to lean into an identity that is bigger than our own limitations.

By feeling thirsty, we learn why it matters that we are salt. By wandering in darkness, we realize how big of a deal it is to be indwelt by light. This process bruises our pride, but some of us have learned to abide in Christ by seeing what happens when we do not.

That was a messy process for me, and messy isn't how I want faith to work. I want a cape of invisibility, a magic wand, a superpower, and six-pack abs. I want to be super-human; after all, Eve's first sin wasn't eating a piece of fruit—she was drawn to a promise that she could be godlike without God. She wasn't trying to be bad; she was trying to be good without her Creator's help or company.

When describing the benefits of discovering human limitations, Bonhoeffer wrote,

> Just as surely as God desires to lead us to a knowledge of genuine Christian fellowship, so surely must we be overwhelmed by a great disillusionment with others, with Christians in general, and, if we are fortunate, with ourselves.
>
> By sheer grace, God will not permit us to live even for a brief period in a dream world. He does not abandon us to those rapturous experiences and lofty moods that come over us like a dream. God is not a God of the emotions but the God of truth. Only that fellowship which faces such

disillusionment, with all its unhappy and ugly aspects, begins to be what it should be in God's sight, begins to grasp in faith the promise that is given to it.[5]

When Those We Love Find Their Underworlds

It's hard enough to go through an underworld of our own, but it's harder still to watch friends or family members experience this sort of darkness. As my oldest kids became teenagers, I began longing for a strategic training program that would defend them from the wicked ways of the world. I had been hurt in the darkness, and I didn't want my children to feel that pain.

Yet, too many theology programs offered to young people are based on logic alone, and a young Christian can't think her way out of a tsunami. When she's dodging broken trees and floating cars—straining against metric tons of water full of jagged edges of metal and wood—she's not going to be working syllogisms in her head. Instead, she'll be coming to terms with her own flesh and bone, the limits of her muscles, the capacity of her lungs.

I have loved my Lord for nearly thirty years, and I've studied theology for many of those years. But when I rely on my apologetic skills to keep my heart steady, I fall quickly to the allure of the world. I suppose this is true for all of us. James K. A. Smith explained why some of our spiritual preparation strategies fall flat in his book *Desiring the Kingdom*:

While Hollister and Starbucks have taken hold of our heart with tangible, material liturgies, Christian schools are "fighting back" by giving young people Christian *ideas*. We hand young people (and old people!) a "Christian worldview" and then tell them, "There, that should fix it." But such strategies are aimed at the head and thus miss the real target: our hearts, our loves, our desires. Christian education as formation needs to be a pedagogy of *desire*.[6]

I wish I knew how to help kids understand desire for the Lord without also learning what it's like to fill their bellies with husks left for the pigs. I don't want young people to take King Solomon's approach, plunging into one futile experiment after another until they finally are exhausted enough to declare, "Vanity, vanity." If I could choose for them, I would give all young believers the way of Enoch, that dear old man who walked small and honest beside God until he woke up one morning and found that he was walking in his eternal presence. What a beautiful way to spend life on earth! *'Tis the gift to be simple, 'tis the gift to be Enoch*, and his is the path I'd want my kids to take if I held the game controls of their lives.

Yet fear and compassion drive me to that desire as much as faith. As much as I hate spiritual disaster, I know God can work with it because so many of my favorite writers have been there. Lewis was an atheist, and he was likely immoral for years. Dorothy Sayers had a child out of wedlock. Chesterton left his childhood faith only to grow madly in love with orthodoxy in the end. Bad choices can leave ugly scars I don't want my children to have; however, God is a master of chasing wandering souls through terrible decisions.

This idea that darkness can be commandeered for good stands fiercely against most of the books I've read on raising kids right, and doing marriages right, and living life right. Methods manuals have filled me with guilt and fear, and some have nearly driven me mad with self-doubt. But as much as I love my children, as much as I'm willing to give to help them, I'm not strong enough to be their savior. God didn't make me their choreographer; he made me their mother. So whether they live robust, trusting lives, or whether they wrestle the Lord until he wins their hearts, I still need the living God to complete what he began in them. If that involves a journey into the underworld, I have to trust the Father to chase them into the valley of the shadow of death.

My husband keeps reminding me that the fatal flaw of most writers is trying to make sense of things before they have come to their proper end; rushing a story is the dark side of the creative nature. But when we try to jerry-rig the natural progression of events God has planned—either in our lives or in the lives of those we love—we aren't trusting him. We are trying to pull the moth out of her cocoon three days too early and then command her to fly when she cannot. We are trying to compress billions of nuances of grace into six tidy paragraphs. We are skimming over our first, giant, reptilian sins; rushing the crude lines of our faith's first cave paintings; reading the CliffsNotes on our early renaissances;

bouncing over our nuclear winters of backsliding; and jumping straight into "They lived happily ever after. The end."

A woman once told me that she broke up with a man because she didn't like the details of their first months together. She had manipulated him early on, and the memories of her greed made her feel ashamed. Her rejection broke the man's heart, but she wanted a clean slate with an idealized story more than she wanted to reconcile the mess of her own reality. So she used him, threw him away, and then moved on—hoping to be a better person in her next relationship. Hearing her explain this sort of consumerism horrified me until I realized I do the same thing in my own ways. I like to finagle the story of my life until it feels good to me.

And yet, freedom waits for the soul who is willing to walk back into the mess of itself, admit the truth, and wait for a real God to move. When we are willing to depend upon a God who lives, forgives, redirects, and upholds, we begin to realize that we don't have to frantically strain to rewrite the meaningless seasons of our lives. We can cling to grace at our center and learn to preach the gospel to ourselves in small, honest ways. The relief of this eternal anchor can lead us to worship, even when the big picture doesn't quite make sense yet.

Making Mass inside the Mess

When I was a teenager, my faith was repeatedly knocked to the earth. Pastors who led churches I had attended were caught showing porn to teenagers, having affairs, embezzling money, and engaging in kleptomania—there was even a suicide and a murder. Each time another hero was pulled away from me, I tried to get back up again to walk with my God, but deep down, I was wounded. Disappointment in those men and women mixed into disappointment I felt in my own weak character.

On days I felt as if I were drowning in all this, I would drive over to the Catholic basilica. I would pull the doors open and sneak in, clumsily genuflecting, then sliding into the pew to pour my heart out to God. The physical act of kneeling felt good after working so hard to be vulgar and violent. The formal beauty of that cathedral was therapeutic in a crass and deformed world.

Behind me were rows of candles folks would light, praying for their beloved deceased. I didn't believe in praying for the dead, but there was still something about the intimate silence of that practice that stirred a fierce homesickness inside me.

"Peace of Christ be with you," whispered an older woman, leaving the candles to give me her hand. I took it in mine, feeling her soft, thin skin rolling around on her bones.

"And also with you," I responded, though I wasn't sure if that was the right response.

Thirty years have passed since my adolescence. It's odd that so many hard, old encounters feel so different to me now. I don't remember when I stopped wanting to hide from those older teenage ballplayers and when I started wishing I could have adopted them. When I think about my angry old coach, I feel empathy toward him instead of just fear and anger. I also see that I misunderstood Jesus' expectations of me. When he said that he wanted his followers to be innocent, he wasn't asking us to be moral perfectionists. He was asking us to realize who he has already made us at the core.

I couldn't have seen any of this thirty years ago, or even twenty. Time had to pass before I could know what God was doing—I had to experience more failure, more loneliness, and more desperation before I could begin to see how the story was being worked into a plot. There was no way to rush the lesson. Growth took time, and it took a long time.

If your situation feels meaningless, it could be that you are still in the middle of things. This season could hold the tension—the strain of achy, dissonant minor chords—that must be played before a resolution. Do you ever get wrapped up in your mistakes, worrying about their consequences and trying to figure out how you can avoid making them again? While it's good to grow, obsessive nervousness can actually distract you from what weakness always reveals—a deep need for union with God.

Our enemy hates the union we have with God more than anything, so he will do whatever he can to keep us from enjoying that closeness. Every whisper in our ears, every nudge trying to get us to steal and cheat is an attempt to lure us away from the beautiful, burning company of God. Temptation works to pull us from greater joys into lesser joys that fade—joys that never satisfy us as God's presence can. Then, once we have sinned, an even greater attack comes.

The enemy switches to strategies of shame and self-effort, pulling us far away from the abiding life in Christ.

In *The Horse and His Boy*, a young orphan boy named Shasta grows discouraged after being pushed to run all night through a dark wood. In his exhaustion, he looks over the futility of his own short life and cries out to a strange Thing that is following him in the blackness,

> "Oh, I am the unluckiest person in the whole world!"
>
> Once more he felt the warm breath of the Thing on his hand and face. "There," it said, "that is not the breath of a ghost. Tell me your sorrows."
>
> Shasta was a little reassured by the breath: so he told how he had never known his real father or mother and had been brought up sternly by the fisherman. And then he told the story of his escape and how they were chased by lions and forced to swim for their lives; and of all their dangers in Tashbaan and about his night among the tombs and how the beasts howled at him out of the desert. And he told about the heat and thirst of their desert journey and how they were almost at their goal when another lion chased them and wounded Aravis. And also, how very long it was since he had had anything to eat.
>
> "I do not call you unfortunate," said the Large Voice.

"Don't you think it was bad luck to meet so many lions?" said Shasta.

"There was only one lion," said the Voice.

"What on earth do you mean? I've just told you there were at least two the first night, and—"

"There was only one: but he was swift of foot."

"How do you know?"

"I was the lion." And as Shasta gaped with open mouth and said nothing, the Voice continued. "I was the lion who forced you to join with Aravis. I was the cat who comforted you among the houses of the dead. I was the lion who drove the jackals from you while you slept. I was the lion who gave the Horses the new strength of fear for the last mile so that you should reach King Lune in time. And I was the lion you do not remember who pushed the boat in which you lay, a child near death, so that it came to shore where a man sat, wakeful at midnight, to receive you."[7]

Although Lewis wrote *The Horse and His Boy* for children, this story didn't connect with me when I was twenty. In fact, I used to think it an outlier in the Narnia series—the plot that connected least with what Lewis was trying to accomplish overall. At forty-five, however, I think it might be the center of every story Lewis tells. The King has been chasing me, comforting me, urging me onward all my life. While I walked through the catalpa trees, longing to balance the new-found weight of a frightening world, my spirit was reaching for its God-given poise. When I found places to kneel amid a culture that swaggered and throat-punched, my spirit was reaching for an eternity of artisan focus. When I felt sharp homesickness—even while the bus tires jolted and shuddered with the angry roar of the losing coach—I was reaching for my heavenly hearth in a noisy, messy world. I never had simplicity or innocence, but I was given saints and pilgrims along the way, authors who extended their bare, bony hands to me while whispering, "The peace of Christ be with you."

"And also with you," I respond.

"Lift up your hearts to the Lord," asks this cloud of witnesses.

"It is right to give him thanks and praise," I say. Glory be to the author and perfecter of our souls.

Father, all-powerful and ever-living God, we do well always and everywhere to give you thanks through Jesus Christ our Lord. Through his cross and resurrection, he freed us from sin and death and called us to the glory that has made us a chosen race, a royal priesthood, a holy nation, a people set apart. Everywhere we proclaim your mighty works for you have called us out of darkness into your own wonderful light. And so, with all the choirs of angels in heaven, we proclaim your glory and join in their unending hymn of praise:

Holy, holy, holy Lord, God of power and might, heaven and earth are full of your glory. Hosanna in

the highest. Blessed is He who comes in the name of the
Lord. Hosanna in the highest.[8]

Father, you are holy indeed, and all creation rightly
gives you praise. All life, all holiness comes from you
through your Son, Jesus Christ, our Lord, by the working
of the Holy Spirit. From age to age you gather a people
to yourself, so that from east to west a perfect offering
may be made to the glory of your name.[9]

All Things New:
A Letter to the Homesick

We had just finished unfolding our soccer chairs at Shakespeare in the Park. Outdoor theater is my favorite entertainment, so as I sat down to wait, I let out a long and happy sigh. This was going to be a good night.

After spreading out a blanket and some food, I opened my phone to post a picture on Facebook—but something in the feed caught my eye. A friend in London had marked himself safe. I clicked on his page. "Got over the bridge just minutes before the attack began," he said.

"It's happened again," I whispered to my husband.

"What's happened?" he asked.

"Terrorists killed a bunch of people in London."

I pulled up the news and saw the pictures you'd expect. Ambulances. Streets full of running men. Images of women standing dazed. An early report suggested that one man had been eating dinner when he was stabbed in the face—just a casual evening out relaxing with friends, and then . . . My stomach felt sick.

They could show up here, I thought. The openness of the park suddenly felt so vulnerable, and the casual, chatty spirit of the crowd seemed naive. I looked around to see if anybody looked suspicious. I wondered how many of my children I could cover with my body if shooting broke out.

Statistically, it wasn't going to happen, and I knew that. The bad guys can't be everywhere at once. But terrorists have borrowed a strategy from the enemy of our souls: *Terrify a million by hurting a few.* Evil seeks out critical pressure points that trigger an avalanche of fear and despair.

All three of our children were together in one place, something that happens rarely now that college is rolling. It wasn't a day to be wasted, so I made the same decision I try to make every time I hear about one of these attacks—the decision to keep on living.

Behind us, an older couple talked about the weather. A two-year-old boy in a bright blue dinosaur hoodie was stomping from blanket to blanket, rawring at us. He was cute, and he knew he was. We rawred back. Strangers were joking with strangers, sharing containers of food and drink. The girl to my right had blue-and-purple hair. A couple of thirtysomethings with funky glasses were digging hummus out of a glass bowl. Four dogs on slack leashes were used to going everywhere with their owners; they raised their noses to sniff the air, then fell back asleep. Halcyon moms breastfed fat, barefoot babies.

Four grass terraces led down to the stage, and they made a patchwork of woven blankets, punctuated by sandals tossed off and bare legs stretched out. Men in slides were walking leisurely, saying, "Pardon me," while holding tiny plastic cups of wine so full that liquid sloshed over the edges with every step. Couples wearing flannel shirts ate grain salads and fresh fruit. Friends with hair pulled into messy knots broke homemade currant scones. A lace scarf. A bow tie. Pajama pants. I smelled Chardonnay and newsprint from the playbill. The tang of bug spray. Someone wasn't wearing deodorant. Someone else smelled like cloves.

Here were children with happy, unbridled manners, academics, vagabonds, and Shakespeare junkies. Here were mathy boyfriends dragged into the arts by bookish girlfriends. The poor and the patrons, we all felt the tickle of expectation that comes before the gift of live theater.

"Fifteen minutes to curtain."

The man beside me told me about his hip surgery. I found the actress who played Beatrice years ago—the feisty one— and we cracked a few jokes. We chewed the fat as if nothing terrible were going on anywhere, then we made it through five acts untouched. But the next morning, I woke up with the world's bad news on my heart again because I can't ever seem to push terror away very long. Like aftershocks, the horrors return. You don't move past news like this with one decision but with a hundred.

In chapter 30 of C. S. Lewis's *The Screwtape Letters*, the wicked demon Screwtape addresses the fatigue of living in violent times like ours. His human target (a young believer) is surviving a war in which there are daily bomb raids that cause constant fear. Screwtape gives his nephew Wormwood two tips on maximizing this external pressure. First, the human must be convinced that every air raid will be his last one: "If I can just survive this awful night, the bombings will stop." False hope like this causes every new attack to snowball into emotional exhaustion. Second, the human must be tricked into setting limits for how long he can "take it." When the bombings go beyond those limits, the human will feel justi-fied in abandoning hope—even though (in truth) he is very close to the finish line.

Lewis published this book in 1942, but many of my friends are feeling a similar gravity right now. We might not be living in the middle of bomb raids, but twenty-four-hour violence runs on the news, there's intense discord in the church and government, and we endure all sorts of verbal violence on the Internet. *It will be over once the election dies down*, we think. Or, *I can't take this intensity for another four years.* But on and on it goes. The ache never stops.

In February of 2017, the American Psychological Association reported that stress rates in America jumped for the first time in ten years.[1] Twelve percent of Americans are on antidepressants, and 8.3 percent are taking drugs including sedatives, hypnotics, and antianxiety medications.[2] Millions more suffer from depression and anxiety without being treated. Drug overdoses in America made the largest jump ever recorded in 2016; this is now the leading cause of death in Americans under 50.[3] So many people are hurting and scared, and we aren't quite sure how to manage all that pain. The last time I visited my doctor, he told me that many of his patients are struggling with news-related anxiety. They are having panic attacks, trouble sleeping, blood pressure issues. All is not right with the world, and we know it.

This Disenchanted World

Three years ago, I was at one of those earthy grocery stores, sitting in a booth, sipping on a paper cup full of Earl Grey with milk. The regular Saturday crowd was filing through. Two female college students walked past my seat, long in the legs, with chiseled cheekbones and chins. They had a Denver sort of outdoor beauty that looks best without being made up.

A young mom and dad walked in, dragging in two sleepy children. The whole family stopped inside the sliding door for a moment, getting their bearings and letting the sun fade out of their eyes. The daughter was maybe four years old, pretty with long black hair mussed over as it does when you sit up from a pillow.

The mom leaned toward the dad, and she said loudly enough that I could hear it, "Hayden. Needs. To. Pee. Right now. He can't wait." Dad threw the boy over his shoulder and headed to the back of the store.

He passed an older man wearing cataract sunglasses and a cardigan who was slowly pushing a cart with nothing inside it.

On the wall of my booth hung a framed photograph of an abandoned redbrick church. It was a tiny little building, too boxy to hold anything more than a sanctuary. I couldn't tell what color the metal roof had been before it turned to rust and rotting leaves. The steeple had a board missing on its left side, which looked like a gap left by a lost tooth. Weeds were grown up all around the yard, jagged stalks of grasses so dry and brittle that even the sunlight falling on them felt severe.

Three trees were growing into the church, pressing themselves against bricks. It hurt to watch this slow pressure. I wanted to find a saw to cut them down, then find an iron bar and pry one of the windows free. I wanted to watch the sanctuary open up like a wide, brown lap because I felt as though if I could just get inside this place, I would be seven years old again.

I don't remember many of the sermons I heard growing up, but I do remember how it felt to be inside a church as a little girl—a tiny little being swallowed up by a hushed and holy room. I remember the communal sigh of two hundred happy bodies settling into creaking wooden pews after standing to sing and the tinkling of glass Communion cups being stacked in reverence. Those churches always smelled like boxwoods, and potluck dinners, and old people wearing rose powder, and hundred-year-old-varnish.

We lived in Ohio in 1977. People there had last names like Zimmerman and Schneider, and their yards were always clean. Old ladies cut their gray hair short, and they didn't hug strangers like big-bosomed western Kentucky women who kissed you whether you were related to them or not. Still, the Ohio women made homemade egg noodles and snickerdoodles, and I liked them well enough.

On Sundays, Mom and Dad would pack my brother and me into a green Ford pickup and drive a mile or two down the road to a white wooden church. A warm, brown portrait of Jesus hung behind the baptismal, an Anglo Jesus instead of a proper Middle Eastern face, but I didn't think about things like that back then. I loved that Jesus because his eyes looked kind, and I wanted to talk to him.

I used to think that if I stared at that picture long enough without blinking, he would move his lips, but my eyes grew heavy from staring and sitting, and after half an hour, I would stretch out long on the wooden pew while the stained-glass windows spattered pink-and-yellow light across my legs like handfuls of thrown confetti. It was disrespectful to let your shoes touch the pews, so I'd kick my Mary Janes off and fall asleep in my sock feet.

There were two metal handrails on the porch behind the church, but I wasn't allowed to flip over them in a skirt because that wasn't ladylike. A large slab of concrete was covered in Astroturf, and during a youth night, I once sat with some teenagers and spat slick, black watermelon seeds into the grass.

I was maybe seven that summer when two laughing dea-
cons grabbed me up off the bank of a church picnic, telling
my mom they were going to teach me how to swim in a lake.
They promised not to let me drown, but I remember being
thrown in before I could catch a full breath, then sinking fast
into the green deep, looking up through what felt like miles
of dark water.

The whole thing was a blur. My giggly kicking in protest,
my flight, the sudden muffle of water in my ears, my flailing,
my resignation, my paralysis. I looked up toward the light as
I fell, and I saw the sun breaking into shards on the surface
through the cold.

I'm drowning, I thought, and then in the same half a heartbeat, I noticed how beautiful the light was a million miles
away on the surface. The presence of beauty at that moment
shocked me. I was going to die, and the world would go
right on being lovely, even while I was being ripped out of
it. Planet Earth didn't care if I was here or not.

Just then, two hands grabbed my waist and pulled me
back up to the air, where I sputtered and gagged, regaining
all my fires of injustice. I punched those men hard in their
bare shoulders, trying to laugh instead of cry because they
were friends of my parents. But I was embarrassed, and I was
shaken. The whole thing had taken two minutes start to finish, but the fright of it had taught me that I could die, and
that the universe wouldn't flinch if I did.

Stephen Crane's "The Open Boat" tells a similar story.
Four men have survived a shipwreck, and they are floating in

a dinghy, out in the open sea. The dinghy is too small to bear them, and after hours of bailing water, fighting to survive, Crane shows us that the world is indifferent to the men's survival. He wrote, "When it occurs to a man that nature does not regard him as important, and that she feels she would not maim the universe by disposing of him, he at first wishes to throw bricks at the temple, and he hates deeply the fact that there are no bricks and no temples."[4] That anger swells up in us because something about an uncaring universe feels wrong. Maybe you've heard an atheist say, "When I first lost my faith, I was angry at God for not existing," and that conclusion makes sense because our instincts tell us that our lives matter in some relational, eternal way. Just as a newborn baby cries out for milk he has never tasted, the human soul arrives on this planet needing to be known intimately—needing to belong somewhere permanent, beautiful, safe, and personal.

The German language uses the word *Sehnsucht* to describe this feeling. It's a word that means "longing" or "craving." *Sehnsucht* is a feeling that you are missing something you love dearly but cannot quite explain to anyone, not even fully to yourself. It is yearning for an ideal that floats always in the peripheral vision of your soul, but it disappears every time you turn and try to look at it. *Sehnsucht* is puttering through vulgar, mundane struggles, missing a home you cannot quite reach, and at the same time longing for a far-off land you have never seen. It is wanting to be in a place you cannot name, though whatever "it" is feels familiar. It is wishing to talk to someone dear to you but not knowing who that is. It is desire, but what is desired can't quite be defined.

C. S. Lewis described *Sehnsucht* as the "inconsolable longing"[5] in the human heart for "we know not what."[6] In the afterword to the third edition of *The Pilgrim's Regress*, he said it was "that unnameable something, desire for which pierces us like a rapier at the smell of a bonfire, the sound of wild ducks flying overhead, the title of *The Well at the World's End*, the opening lines of *Kubla Khan*, the morning cobwebs in late summer, or the noise of falling waves."[7] This longing eventually won the soul of the "most dejected and reluctant convert in all England."[8] Lewis was a rationalist, a materialist, and a hardened atheist when he ran into beauty more powerful than all his resistance. He finally had to admit that he was hungry with a hunger that would not leave him alone—thanks be to God.

Many of us have felt that homesickness at one point or another, but pain, disappointment, and stress wear us down over time. We get tired of longing for what feels so distant, tired of running an invisible race toward an invisible goal, so we start to settle for immediate comforts that we can scrounge up in the here and now.

Pastors warn Christians about the allure of the pleasures of the world, but if we could see the joys of earth and the joys of eternity clearly contrasted against one another, the materialist would seem more slothful than extravagant. He would look like a man ordering a McRib in the drive-through when a home-cooked feast waits five miles down the road. Giving up on faith is a product of laziness as much as rebellion, and the atheist battle cry is not the roar of a Balrog so much as the sounds of a couch potato sucking Dorito cheese off his fingertips. In his other hand, he's holding not a wizard's wand but a remote control, flipping through reruns of *Three's Company*. As Lewis concluded, "We are far too easily pleased."[9]

The Courage to Ache for the Unseen

I understand this default to passivity because I've embraced it many times myself. In grueling seasons of pain, I've checked out of the marathon of faith and collapsed into some sort of easy, physical diversion. Online shopping, stupid humor, food, Twitter spats—again and again, I've lost myself in low pleasures that promised a few moments of relief.

Our world generally applauds such diversions as pain management strategies. We joke about drinking too much wine on bad parenting days or medicating political stress by chocolate therapy. Men and women who grieve too much or too loudly are labeled "snowflakes," often by men with egos even more fragile than those they accuse. So there's a comic irony to it all—neither the heat-packing tough guys nor the uber-feelers seem to manage the intensity of a broken earth with holy balance.

We struggle to keep perspective because seeing into eternity is difficult. Screwtape's human stumbles while watching the carnage of war, and Lewis allows us to watch him attempt to process violence in a way that makes some sort of sense. The master demon says to his protégé,

> Probably the scenes he [the human] is now witnessing will not provide material for an intellectual attack on his faith—your previous failures have put that out of your power. *But there is a sort of attack on the emotions which can still be tried. It turns on making him feel, when first he sees human remains plastered on a wall, that this is 'what the world is really like' and that all his religion has been a fantasy.*[10]

Don't you ever feel this temptation in our era of the street terrorist? When you see peaceful scenes turned into bloody panic, do you wonder if humans are nothing more than animals after all?

In such dark times, we need the romance of the Bible as much as we need its linear proofs. Frederick Buechner wrote about the gospel in terms of comedy, tragedy, and fairy tale—not because he felt it was untrue but because he recognized that the human heart needs metanarrative.[11] If you watched the 2017 film *Wonder Woman*, you remember that epic scene in which she charges through enemy lines for the sake of the desperate. My heart felt as if it were going to pound out of my chest here because I had forgotten the beauty of the story of selflessness. While modernity tends to elevate the syllogism over the narrative, Jesus leaned heavily into parable when training his followers. James K. A. Smith has described the strategic benefit of this sort of affective vision by stating,

> The reason that this vision of the good life moves us is because it is a more affective, sensible, even aesthetic *picture* of what the good life looks like. A vision of the good life captures our hearts and imaginations not by providing a set of rules or ideas, but by painting a picture of what it looks like for us to flourish and live well. This is why such pictures are communicated most powerfully in stories, legends, myths, plays, novels, and films rather than dissertations, messages, and monographs. Because we are affective before we are cognitive (and even *while* we are cognitive), visions of the good get inscribed in us by means that are commensurate with our primarily affective, imaginative nature. This isn't to say that the cognitive or propositional is a completely foreign register for us (if it were, this book would be an exercise in futility!); however, it doesn't get into our (noncognitive) bones in the same way or with the same effect. The cognitive and propositional is easily reduced and marginalized as just more "blah-blah-blah" when our hearts and imaginations are captured by a more compelling *picture* of the good life.[12]

When filling the Bible with stories, God knew that his people needed a "once upon a time" leading to a "happily ever after." It was not a spiritual accident that led godless deconstructionists like Derrida to attack metanarrative, stripping human hope away from a cardinal plot map that helps tired souls take a few more steps toward a grand finale. It is the inherent work of darkness to hover over order and say, "Let there be chaos." This is why believers must continually look down the line of our faith, into its telos, returning over and again to a good, strong vision of our heavenly hearth. If we don't, we won't be able to endure the discouragement of life here in the shadowlands.

There have been so many times over this past year when my heart was burdened, overwhelmed with all of the hypocrisy and savagery of the world. Desperate, I have come to the Word of God, not just with my mind but with my tired soul, allowing its stories to wash over my soreness and revive my courage.

But it's hard to find thoughtful modern writers who remain faithful to this great romance. In an attempt to correct Rapture-escapist theology of the 1980s and 1990s, writers have thrown their weight behind the social-justice side of Christianity. I've even seen poets and preachers shaming believers for daydreaming about eternity, urging them to get their heads out of the clouds and work hard to bring heaven to earth.

How sad to correct the theological errors of the last generation with a graver error still. Setting service on earth and an ache for heaven in opposition to one another is unhealthy and unbiblical. The New Testament is full of longing for eternity, just as it is full of exhortations to tend the desperate; these two forces are meant to work in sync with one another. They propel one another; they don't compete. Paul's deep desire to depart and be with Christ drove him into focused, compassionate ministry during the years he spent on earth, and this longing should drive us to do the same.

The Courage to See as a Child

We respect the terrestrial most deeply when we dip our souls in the pigments of God's eternal palette. "On earth as it is in heaven," said Jesus because we are vessels created to overflow, designed for a moment-by-moment, trust-borne, indwelt fluidity that is inherently childlike. Children sing when the wind blows; they dance when the music rises; they leap giggling when their fathers call them to fly into strong arms, which is probably why Jesus said, "Truly, I say to you, whoever does not receive the kingdom of God like a child shall not enter it."[13] Adults think and do, but we hesitate to respond.

Addressing the toxic myopia of old age, Chesterton wrote what is possibly his most beautiful chapter of all, "The Ethics of Elfland." It begins like this:

When the business man rebukes the idealism of his office-boy, it is commonly in some such speech as this: "Ah, yes, when one is young, one has these

ideals in the abstract and these castles in the air; but
in middle age they all break up like clouds, and one
comes down to a belief in practical politics, to using
the machinery one has and getting on with the world
as it is." Thus, at least, venerable and philanthropic
old men now in their honoured graves used to talk
to me when I was a boy. But since then I have grown
up and have discovered that these philanthropic old
men were telling lies. What has really happened is
exactly the opposite of what they said would happen.
They said that I should lose my ideals and begin to
believe in the methods of practical politicians. Now,
I have not lost my ideals in the least; my faith in
fundamentals is exactly what it always was. What I
have lost is my old childlike faith in practical politics.
I am still as much concerned as ever about the Battle
of Armageddon; but I am not so much concerned
about the General Election. As a babe I leapt up on
my mother's knee at the mere mention of it. No; the
vision is always solid and reliable. The vision is always
a fact. It is the reality that is often a fraud.[14]

C. S. Lewis seemed to agree. In a letter to his goddaughter
Lucy Barfield, Lewis wrote, "Some day you will be old enough to
start reading fairy tales again."[15] He knew this fact because he had
lived through the change himself. "When I was ten," he wrote,
"I read fairy tales in secret and would have been ashamed if I had
been found doing so. Now that I am fifty I read them openly.

When I became a man I put away childish things, including the fear of childishness and the desire to be very grown up."[16]

These men were not intellectually weak. They had a capacity for logic and philosophy that far exceeds most thinkers of our own time, and both had lived through intense seasons of rebellion from the Christian faith. They spoke as men who knew both sides of the coin. Emerging from the underworld of atheism, the boon they offered the world was an exhortation to childlike trust, a willingness to see beyond the ambivalence of the natural world into the enchantment of creation.

They have challenged a cerebral cynic (like me) to read verses like the following with the wonder of a little girl listening to a fairy tale.

> You will go out in joy
>   and be led forth in peace;
> the mountains and hills
>   will burst into song before you,
> and all the trees of the field
>   will clap their hands.
>
> ISAIAH 55:12, NIV

Here, flora and fauna are awake. Three great, green, Appalachian peaks open sylvan mouths: "Praise God, from whom all blessings flow; Praise him, all creatures here below!"[17] October sugar maples stand giddy as children at an Independence Day parade, smacking their leaves together, shaking one another by the shoulders: "Look there! Look there!"

And when Jesus answers, "I tell you, if these were silent, the very stones would cry out,"[18] I feel permission now to see a marine block of granite rumbling to full salute: "Atten-hut! The Messiah is passing!" Cobblestone babies roll over in their tight little beds and yawn. Pillars of polished marble recite the affirmations of a chorus: "He is the Promised One!"

> For we know that the whole creation has been
> groaning together in the pains of childbirth until now.
> And not only the creation, but we ourselves, who have
> the firstfruits of the Spirit, groan inwardly as we wait
> eagerly for adoption as sons, the redemption of our
> bodies. For in this hope we were saved. Now hope
> that is seen is not hope.[19]

"Who hopes for what they already have?"[20] wrote the apostle Paul, and as I read these words, I feel all creation responding—including my cranky kneecaps ("Come, Lord Jesus"); my quadriceps tendon that whines and shivers ("How much longer?"); that hot left sciatic nerve, my inner wailing Jeremiah. My sagging, middle-aged face sighs into the mirror and recites the story of the Transfiguration.

The Courage to Live in Two Worlds at Once

Sometime during the spring that I was twenty, I needed to walk across campus from the library to my dorm room a few minutes past midnight. The heat of the day had wilted the little viburnum flowers on the bushes in front of the library, and it was almost as if the wilting had released the best oils of their fragrance. Perfume was hanging in the air, a reckless extravagance like wine saved for the end of a wedding feast.

I was nervous to be out alone in the dark, so I bolted past that heady sweetness, then stopped. It was worth the risk. I ran back—half-afraid of being murdered—and I buried my face in those branches and took them in with slow, delicious breaths. As goose bumps rose all over my arms, I knew that I wanted whatever this longing signified. God was preparing a place for my restless heart, and somehow these viburnums pointed home.

Memory of that night returns to me whenever I reread George MacDonald's book *Lilith*, a story of a man who takes a journey into parallel worlds. MacDonald's two realms overlap so that a piano room in one might look like a field of wild hyacinth in another. In glimpses, the protagonist can see those intersections like a Christian who looks with the eyes of faith.

Paul's letter to the Ephesians tells us that in some mysterious way, we are already seated in the heavenlies, which means every present move of our hearts somehow fits into an eternal trajectory. When we clean the toilets, we are seated in the heavenlies. When we write a Facebook post, we are seated in the heavenlies. When we feel worn out from one more painful misunderstanding, we are seated in the heavenlies. Everything we do here is so significant.

I don't know if modern physicists are correct about string

theory, but the idea of overlapping, invisible dimensions doesn't originate in science. For thousands of years, the Lord has been showing us that multiple layers of reality coincide. In 2 Kings, Elisha asks God to open the eyes of his servant so that he might see a mountain full of horses and chariots of fire. "And behold," the text says, because it is always a wonder to have the limitations of human perception pulled away like a curtain and to be given a straight, clear vision into the spiritual realm.[21]

This passage reads like the climax of a child's novel, a glimpse into an enchanted world. "A mountain full of horses and chariots of fire!" we think, looking around at the walls of our rooms, holding our breath like kids who can't sleep before Christmas morning. "And behold!" we whisper, feeling a resurgence of courage to ask for God to move in those unseen valleys where our dearest battles are fought.

Those of us who witness senseless horrors are tempted to grant evil permission to become ultimate truth, but this is too much ground to give the operatives of hell. Simultaneous realities exist for us, but not all realities are equal.

One thread of action runs on the world's stage—in the hard lives of strangers sitting beside us, in blasts of random violence that sometimes hit too close, in the broken stories of our own lives. But also, a higher script is being read, whispered in the flutter of leaves on a lazy June evening. It rings from old hymns, and old stories, and old earth. We see what is, then we see what is also—and the latter makes us better at living in the former.

You have a spirit that is woven from the fabric of the new creation. The core of you is formed so that your deepest, truest longing is for intimacy with God. Realizing this is powerful because it helps you see that who you already are reaches instinctively for what is to come. Understanding this new nature can allow you to cast off the sin that so easily entangles and run with endurance.

If you choose to embrace this reality, you will be opposed at every turn. Nothing could be more dangerous to our enemy than your willingness to live in the here and now with the unseen power of your new identity, with your eyes set like dear little Reepicheep's on Aslan's country. And yet, doesn't your heart pound when you consider his resolve?

> My own plans are made. While I can, I sail east in the *Dawn Treader*. When she fails me, I paddle east in my coracle. When she sinks, I shall swim east with my four paws. And when I can swim no longer, if I have not reached Aslan's country, or shot over the edge of the world in some vast cataract, I shall sink with my nose to the sunrise.[22]

To sink with our noses to the sunrise, dear hearts. To paddle a little coracle to Aslan's country. To see with the eyes of a child, peering into two worlds at once. This is the courage we must have. All the forces of hell may come against you, but they will not prevail against the church of God; our eternity comes soon—so very soon—and we will co-reign with

Jesus. But before we can dance with a partner, we must learn to trust him.

You are homesick, and I am too. But we will not be so weary always. We know the end of this story, see. We are very nearly there, in fact. Just a breath. Just a few more days of broken hearts—just a twinkling of the eye, and then,

> I saw a new heaven and a new earth, for the first heaven and the first earth had passed away, and the sea was no more. And I saw the holy city, new Jerusalem, coming down out of heaven from God, prepared as a bride adorned for her husband.
>
> And I heard a loud voice from the throne saying, "Behold, the dwelling place of God is with man. He will dwell with them, and they will be his people, and God himself will be with them as their God. He will wipe away every tear from their eyes, and death shall be no more, neither shall there be mourning, nor crying, nor pain anymore, for the former things have passed away."
>
> And he who was seated on the throne said, "Behold, I am making all things new."[23]

Notes

LETTER 1—HULLO, OUT THERE!: A NOTE TO THE READER

1. Janice Shaw Crouse, "The Loneliness of American Society," *American Spectator*, May 18, 2014, https://spectator.org/59230_loneliness-american-society/.
2. 1 Thessalonians 5:16.
3. Philippians 1:22-23, BSB. Emphasis added.
4. Matthew 26:38, NIV.
5. Matthew 26:39.
6. Luke 22:42, KJV.
7. C. S. Lewis, *The Voyage of the* Dawn Treader (New York, NY: HarperTrophy, 2000), 186.
8. Lewis, *Voyage*, 187.

LETTER 2—I KNOW A STRANGER: A LETTER TO THE REJECTED

1. This retelling of the Leah/Rachel narrative is fictional, not intended to be exegetical. For the actual story, read the book of Genesis.
2. Paraphrase of Ephesians 2:8-9.
3. Song of Solomon 1:6.
4. Song of Solomon 2:13-14.
5. C. S. Lewis, *The Chronicles of Narnia* (New York, NY: HarperCollins, 2001), 185.
6. Gilbert K. Chesterton, *Orthodoxy* (New York: John Lane Company, 1908), 89.
7. Romans 5:8.
8. John 18:40, NIV.
9. Isaiah 53:2-4.
10. See 1 John 4:10.

11. Ephesians 1:4.

LETTER 3—BIRD WITH A BROKEN WING: A LETTER TO THE LONG-SUFFERING

1. Tim Keller, "God Is Bigger Than Our Fears—Praying Our Fears, Psalm 3:1-8," Sermon Notes, September 28, 2014, fpcwickenburg.org/app/download /7116612748/9-28-14+Sermon+Notes.docx.
2. Job 38:3-4, NIV.
3. John 11:21-22, NRSV.
4. John 11:32, NRSV.
5. John 11:33.
6. See 2 Corinthians 1:8.
7. Psalm 22:29, NIV.
8. See Matthew 11:30.
9. See Psalm 3:3.
10. See Psalm 51:17.
11. See James 4:6.
12. Isaiah 42:3.
13. Sara Lentati, "The Man Who Cut Out His Own Appendix," *BBC News*, May 5, 2015, http://www.bbc.com/news/magazine-32481442.
14. Galatians 3:3.
15. John 15:5.

LETTER 4—PROTEIN SOUP: A LETTER TO THOSE LIVING IN CHAOS

1. Amy Carmichael, *Edges of His Ways: Daily Devotional Notes* (Fort Washington, PA: CLC Publications, 2011), 139. Emphasis added.
2. Rich Mullins, "We Are Not As Strong As We Think We Are," *Songs*, copyright © 1996, Reunion Records, Inc.
3. Ruth Myers with Warren Myers, *31 Days of Praise: Enjoying God Anew* (Colorado Springs, CO: Multnomah Books, 1994), 72.
4. 2 Corinthians 12:8-9, NIV.
5. 2 Corinthians 12:9-10, NIV.
6. 2 Corinthians 12:10, NIV.
7. Galatians 2:20.
8. John 15:5-7.
9. Galatians 2:20.
10. 2 Corinthians 4:7, KJV.
11. 2 Corinthians 3:9-11.
12. 2 Corinthians 4:16-17, NASB.

13. Sally Lloyd-Jones, *The Jesus Storybook Bible: Every Story Whispers His Name* (Grand Rapids, MI: Zonderkidz, 2012), 14–17.
14. 2 Corinthians 5:2-4, NIV.

LETTER 5—SCARED TO DEATH: A LETTER TO THE FEARFUL
1. Sean M. Smith and Wylie W. Vale, "The Role of the Hypothalamic-Pituitary-Adrenal Axis in Neuroendocrine Responses to Stress," *Dialogues in Clinical Neuroscience* 8, no. 4 (December 2006): 383–95, https://www.ncbi.nlm.nih.gov/pmc/articles/PMC3181830/.
2. Smith and Vale, "Role of the Hypothalamic-Pituitary-Adrenal Axis."
3. Smith and Vale, "Role of the Hypothalamic-Pituitary-Adrenal Axis."
4. Thierry Steimer, "The Biology of Fear- and Anxiety-Related Behaviors," *Dialogues in Clinical Neuroscience* 4, no. 3 (September 2002): 231–49, https://www.ncbi.nlm.nih.gov/pmc/articles/PMC3181681/.
5. Lewis references this concept in his essay "Miracles." See C. S. Lewis, "Miracles," in *God in the Dock: Essays on Theology and Ethics* (Grand Rapids, MI: Eerdmans, 2014), 13–15.
6. Andrew Peterson, "More," *The Far Country*, copyright © 2005, Word Entertainment.
7. Daniela McVicker, "Recent Research Links Anxiety with Higher IQ," *World of Psychology* (blog), *PsychCentral*, July 26, 2017, https://psychcentral.com/blog/recent-research-links-anxiety-with-higher-iq/.
8. David Wilson, "Scary Smart," *Slate*, April 15, 2015, http://www.slate.com/articles/health_and_science/science/2015/04/do_smart_people_worry_more_iq_is_correlated_with_anxiety.html.
9. John 1:14, NIV.
10. C. S. Lewis, *The Screwtape Letters* (New York: HarperOne, 2001), 39–40. Emphasis added.
11. See Jeremiah 6:14-15.
12. Philippians 4:7, NIV.
13. Isaiah 41:10, HCSB. Emphasis added.
14. 1 John 4:18. Emphasis added.
15. Matthew 10:31, NIV. Emphasis added.
16. Corrie ten Boom, *Each New Day: 365 Reflections to Strengthen Your Faith* (Grand Rapids, MI: Revell, 2013), 78.

LETTER 6—THE KISS OF THE MOUNTAIN GOD: A LETTER TO THE SKEPTICAL
1. Rich Mullins, "Calling Out Your Name," *The World As Best As I Remember It*, vol. 1, copyright © 1991, Reunion Records.

2. Wendell Berry, *New Collected Poems* (Berkeley, CA: Counterpoint, 2012), 139.

3. See 2 Samuel 6:14.

4. Referenced in Steve Brown, *Approaching God: Accepting the Invitation to Stand in the Presence of God* (New York, NY: Howard Books, 2008), 110.

5. Chesterton, *Orthodoxy*, 22–23.

6. Robert Farrar Capon, *The Supper of the Lamb: A Culinary Reflection* (Garden City, NY: Doubleday & Company, Inc., 1969), 99.

7. C. S. Lewis, *The Weight of Glory: and Other Addresses* (New York: HarperOne, 2001), 140.

8. Brené Brown, "Listening to Shame," filmed March 2, 2012, in Long Beach, California, TED video, 20:32, https://www.ted.com/talks/brene_brown_listening_to_shame.

9. T. S. Eliot, *Collected Poems: 1909–1962* (Orlando, FL: Harcourt, 1991), 82.

10. If you don't understand this reference, I hope you will go read *The Horse and His Boy* by C. S. Lewis. Trust me. It's worth your time.

LETTER 7—THE WHISPER AT OUR BACKS: A LETTER TO THE DISILLUSIONED

1. Matthew 18:6-7, BSB.

2. NAS Exhaustive Concordance, s.v. "skandalizó," accessed January 19, 2018, http://biblehub.com/greek/4624.htm.

3. Chesterton, *Orthodoxy*, 52–53. Emphasis added.

4. Chesterton, *Orthodoxy*, 65.

5. NAS Exhaustive Concordance, s.v. "mikros," accessed January 19, 2018, http://biblehub.com/greek/3398.htm.

6. Matthew 10:42.

7. Matthew 18:10.

8. Matthew 18:14.

9. Luke 12:32.

10. Revelation 2:3-5, BSB.

11. Victor Hugo, *Les Misérables*, trans. Julie Rose (New York, NY: Modern Library, 2008), 514. Emphasis added.

12. Corrie ten Boom, *The Hiding Place* (New York: Bantam Books, 1971), 201.

13. Lewis, *Screwtape Letters*, 64.

14. Lewis, *Screwtape Letters*, 64.

15. *Frederick* by Leo Lionni.

16. Because I used these memories to help combat disillusionment, I'm only including positive stories here. Negative stories offer lessons of their own, of course, but sometimes those treasures are more difficult to unpack.

17. See Nehemiah 4:16-18.
18. Variations of this theme appear throughout Scripture. For example, see Exodus 34:6, Numbers 14:18, Psalm 86:5, and Psalm 103:8.
19. Paraphrase of Luke 2:11.
20. Jeremiah 29:13, NIV.
21. James K. A. Smith, *Desiring the Kingdom: Worship, Worldview, and Cultural Formation* (Grand Rapids, MI: BakerAcademic, 2009).
22. Smith, *Desiring the Kingdom*, 54.
23. See Luke 5, "Jesus Calls the First Disciples."
24. John 6:35.
25. John 8:12.
26. 1 Kings 19:7-8, CEV.
27. J. R. R. Tolkien, *The Lord of the Rings* (Boston, MA: Houghton Mifflin, 2004), 51.
28. Martin Luther, "A Mighty Fortress Is Our God," 1529, public domain.

LETTER 8—NOT ALL WHO WANDER ARE LOST: A LETTER TO THE EXPAT

1. Joseph Brackett, "Simple Gifts," 1848, public domain.
2. Tolkien, *Lord of the Rings*, 32.
3. Romans 16:19.
4. John 17:15.
5. Dietrich Bonhoeffer, *Dietrich Bonhoeffer: Witness to Jesus Christ*, ed. John W. de Gruchy (Minneapolis, MN: Fortress Press, 1991), 182.
6. Smith, *Desiring the Kingdom*, 33.
7. C. S. Lewis, *The Horse and His Boy* (New York, NY: HarperCollins, 1994), 163–65.
8. "The Traditional (Tridentine) Missal compared to the Mass of Paul VI (Novus Ordo) Missal," St. Joseph's Catholic Church, accessed January 24, 2018, http://www.stjosephschurch.net/compare.htm. See New Order of Mass, the Preface and the Sanctus.
9. "The Order of the Holy Mass (Prior to 2011)," Catholic Doors Ministry, accessed January 24, 2018, http://www.catholicdoors.com/misc/holymass .htm. See "Eucharistic Prayer III: In Praise to the Father."

LETTER 9—ALL THINGS NEW: A LETTER TO THE HOMESICK

1. David Oliver, "Survey: Stress in America Increases for the First Time in 10 Years," *U.S. News & World Report*, February 15, 2017, http://health .usnews.com/wellness/health-buzz/articles/2017-02-15/survey-stress-in -america-increases-for-the-first-time-in-10-years.

2. Sara G. Miller, "1 in 6 Americans Takes a Psychiatric Drug," *Scientific American*, December 13, 2016, https://www.scientificamerican.com /article/1-in-6-americans-takes-a-psychiatric-drug/.
3. Josh Katz, "Drug Deaths in America Are Rising Faster Than Ever," *New York Times*, June 5, 2017, https://www.nytimes.com/interactive/2017/06 /05/upshot/opioid-epidemic-drug-overdose-deaths-are-rising-faster-than -ever.html?mcubz=0.
4. Stephen Crane, *The Open Boat: And Other Tales of Adventure* (New York: Doubleday & McClure Co., 1898), 44.
5. C. S. Lewis, *Surprised by Joy: The Shape of My Early Life* (Orlando, FL: Harcourt Brace, 1955), 68.
6. Quoted in Lewis, *Surprised by Joy*, 67.
7. C. S. Lewis, *The Pilgrim's Regress* (Grand Rapids, MI: Eerdmans, 2014), 237.
8. Lewis, *Surprised by Joy*, 221.
9. Lewis, *The Weight of Glory*, 26.
10. Lewis, *Screwtape Letters*, 167. Emphasis added.
11. Frederick Buechner, *Telling the Truth: The Gospel as Tragedy, Comedy, and Fairy Tale* (San Francisco, CA: HarperSanFrancisco, 1977), 106.
12. Smith, *Desiring the Kingdom*, 53–54.
13. Mark 10:15.
14. Chesterton, *Orthodoxy*, 81–82.
15. Lewis, *The Chronicles of Narnia*, 110.
16. C. S. Lewis, "On Three Ways of Writing for Children," accessed February 12, 2018, http://myweb.scu.edu.tw/~jmklassen/scu99b/chlitgrad/3ways.pdf.
17. Thomas Ken, "Praise God, from Whom All Blessings Flow," 1674, public domain.
18. Luke 19:40.
19. Romans 8:22-24.
20. Romans 8:24, NIV.
21. 2 Kings 6:17.
22. Lewis, *Voyage*, 213.
23. Revelation 21:1-5.